backyard BIOLOGY

investigate habitats outside your door

with **25** projects

DONNA LATHAM

Illustrated by Beth Hetland

~ Latest Titles in the *Build It Yourself* Series ~

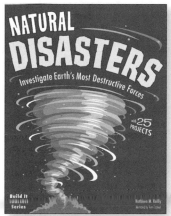

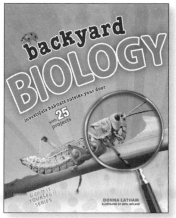

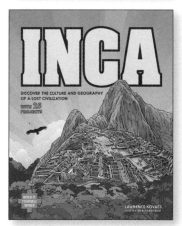

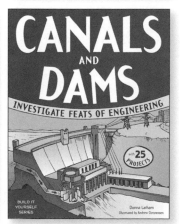

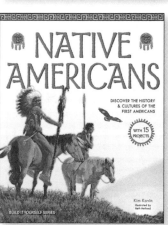

Check out more titles at www.nomadpress.net

green press INITIATIVE

Nomad Press is committed to preserving ancient forests and natural resources. We elected to print *Backyard Biology: Investigate Habitats Outside Your Door* on 4,007 lbs. of Williamsburg Recycled 30% offset.

Nomad Press made this paper choice because our printer, Sheridan Books, is a member of Green Press Initiative, a nonprofit program dedicated to supporting authors, publishers, and suppliers in their efforts to reduce their use of fiber obtained from endangered forests.

For more information, visit **www.greenpressinitiative.org**.

This book was manufactured by Sheridan Books,
Ann Arbor, MI USA.
February 2013, Job #344176
ISBN: 978-1-61930-151-1

Illustrations by Beth Hetland
Educational Consultant Marla Conn

Questions regarding the ordering of this book should be addressed to
Independent Publishers Group
814 N. Franklin St., Chicago, IL 60610
www.ipgbook.com

Nomad Press
2456 Christian St.
White River Junction, VT 05001
www.nomadpress.net

contents

Become a Nature Detective

Life in all its wonder is everywhere. It thrives in the city. It blooms in the country. Life flourishes in deserts, forests, and oceans—even in the Arctic. You can find a place to explore living things almost anywhere you go. But you don't have to go too much farther than right outside your door!

Your own backyard is an ideal place for investigation. Parks, playgrounds, and nature preserves are outdoor science labs. Discover life over your head, under your toes, and all around you. Ask questions, make predictions, and record your observations. Think like a scientist. And have fun connecting with the astonishing natural world.

1

Backyard Biology

Become A Nature Detective

Detectives use special tools of the trade to track down clues and solve mysteries. Assemble your own toolkit to scout for nature clues. Stash supplies in a backpack. Hang it in the same place all the time, so it's always ready and waiting. Include binoculars to study living things that are far away. A magnifying glass is perfect for zooming in on critters up close. Add a small garden shovel and some old spoons for collecting soil samples. Recycle plastic containers with lids to store samples. As you work with your toolkit, you can add other supplies you might need to investigate nature.

After you assemble your Nature Detective toolkit, choose an outdoor area to investigate. What living and nonliving things can you identify? How do you know what's alive and what isn't?

Toss in a science journal and pencils to record and sketch observations. Using a scientific method worksheet will help you keep your ideas and observations organized. The scientific method is the way that scientists ask questions and then find answers.

Scientific Method Worksheet

Our Questions:
Our Equipment:
Method: (What did we do?)
My Predictions: (What I think will happen)
Results: (What happened and WHY)

About the Projects

Life is all around you! Use the projects and activities in this book to tap into your curiosity about the living world. Most projects involve the **ecosystems** that are outside your door—whether it's right in your own backyard, in a neighborhood park or playground, or in a nature preserve. You'll put together a Nature Detective toolkit to scout out clues to investigate life. Along the way you'll discover why **cells** are called life's building blocks and explore the invisible world of **microorganisms**. And you'll learn about the **life cycles** of a **diverse** world of plants and animals.

Words to Know

ecosystem: a community of living and nonliving things and their **environments**.

environment: everything in nature, living and nonliving, including animals, plants, rocks, soil, and water.

cell: the basic unit or part of a living thing. Cells are so small they can only be seen with a microscope.

microorganism: a tiny living thing, such as bacteria, that can only be seen with a microscope. Also called a microbe.

life cycle: the growth and changes a living thing goes through, from birth to death.

diverse: lots of different kinds.

Did you know...

How diverse are living things? Consider the world's smallest and tallest dogs! Pint-sized Boo Boo, a toy Chihuahua from Kentucky, stands a wee 4 inches high (10 centimeters), about as tall as a soft-drink can. At birth, she was the size of a flash drive! Gibson, a Great Dane from California, towers head-and-shoulders over Boo Boo—and then some. He's 3 feet, 6 inches tall (107 centimeters). Measure against a doorframe to check out Gibson's height.

Most projects in this book involve items you might have around the house. They use paper plates, shoeboxes, 2-liter bottles, ziplock bags, newspaper, brown bags, etc. Some require modeling clay, gelatin, dried pasta, bean seeds, and Epsom salts. If you don't have all the listed materials and supplies needed for a project, think of what you can use as a substitute. Borrow or trade materials with a friend.

Of course, you already know safety's first. So ask an adult for help when handling materials such as raw eggs and rubbing alcohol. Don't use the oven or sharp objects by yourself. Pay attention to the safety warnings at the beginning of some of the projects. Before you explore outside, team up with an adult to identify and list safety rules to follow.

Leaves of three? Let 'em be!

This old rhyme warns against poison ivy and poison oak. When touched, these poisonous plants trigger allergic reactions. They cause splotchy rashes, terrible itching, and blisters. Learn about poisonous plants that grow in your area. Find out what they look like so you can identify and avoid touching these plants.

Planet Protector

Exploring the outdoors is a fantastic opportunity for discovery. And it's a chance to pitch in and protect the planet. Respect nature as you explore it by treating it gently. Try to avoid actions that could cause any harm.

Chapter 1

The Study of Life

Biology is the study of life and living **organisms.** Earth boasts a mind-boggling **diversity** of life and ecosystems. But all life on Earth is connected. Life forms range from invisible microorganisms squirming under your thumbnail to gigantic blue whales swimming in oceans.

Words to Know

biology: the study of life and of living organisms.

organism: a living thing, such as a plant or animal.

diversity: a range of different things.

Earth's **species** are so varied and plentiful, it's tricky to identify how many there are. According to the National Science Foundation, scientists have named and recorded 1.8 million species. They are always finding new species and some believe Earth's total number may be closer to 10 million.

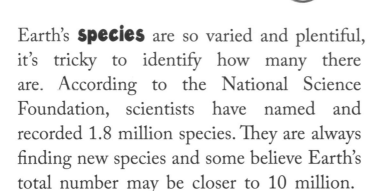

Words to Know

species: a group of plants or animals that are closely related and look the same.

conservationist: a person who works to preserve nature.

In 2007, for example, a research team discovered an amazing new species in the foothills of Cambodia's Cardamon Mountains. An olive-colored gecko with yellowish splotches and a v-shaped pattern marking its scaly skin blended so well against its rocky surroundings that scientists nearly missed it. In 2010, scientists named the gecko "Cnemaspis neangthyi" to honor Neang Thy, a Cambodian **conservationist**.

Did you know...

The prefix "bio" means "life." The suffix "ology" means "the study of."

Earth added a new named species to its booming total number.

The Largest Animal On Earth

What animal has a gargantuan heart the weight of a small car? And a monster tongue the weight of an elephant? The blue whale, the largest animal that has ever lived on Earth! Babies, called calves, measure about 23 feet at birth (7 meters). Massive males grow to a whopping length of 82 feet (25 meters). Females are even more gigantic. They rule the waves at 110 feet long (33½ meters).

Bountiful Biology

Will you discover a new species? As a backyard **biologist**, you'll explore three different branches of biology.

Microbiology is the study of microorganisms. Micro means small. Microorganisms are so tiny they can't be seen with the human eye alone. To view them, people need microscopes. **Botany** is the study of plants. Plants are essential to the natural world. They help make life on Earth possible.

Zoology is the study of animals. Like plants, animals **adapt** to the world around them. The Cambodian gecko **camouflaged** itself against surrounding trees and rocks. It disappeared as if wearing an invisibility cloak. Other animals develop behaviors and physical traits necessary for survival. What **adaptations** will you observe in your backyard adventures?

Words to Know

biologist: a scientist who studies life.

microbiology: the study of microorganisms.

botany: the study of plants.

zoology: the study of animals.

adapt: to change to survive in new or different conditions.

camouflage: the use of colors or patterns to blend in with a background.

adaptation: the changes a plant or animal has made to help it survive.

Characteristics of Living Things

Microorganisms, plants, and animals are all living things. Take a look at your surroundings. What's alive? A friend sitting next to you? A pet snoozing in your lap? Perhaps a bright green wild parakeet with its long aqua tail is chirping outside. Do you see a jackrabbit sniffing around a prickly pear cactus? Peek around again. What are some nonliving things? What about this book or your e-reader? Are you sitting at a desk or table, or with a laptop? Outside, you might see soil and rocks.

Sometimes it's tricky to tell the difference between living and nonliving things. Imagine that parakeet and the prickly pear cactus.

They don't seem much alike, do they? A parakeet is an animal. A cactus is a plant. But both are alive.

Living things on Earth can be wildly different from each other. How can you tell when an organism is alive? All living things share common characteristics.

- Living things are made up of one or more cells.

- Living things need energy to survive.

- Living things grow, develop, and die.

- Living things **reproduce**, or have babies.

- Living things respond to what's around them in their environments.

- Livings things adapt to survive in their environments.

Words to Know

reproduce: to make something new, just like itself. To have babies.

Every living thing has a life cycle. Living organisms are born. As they develop, they grow and change. They reproduce. In time they die. Consider a parakeet's life cycle. It grows in an egg its mother laid.

Life Cycle

After pecking out of its shell, the tiny chick is very weak. The chick can hardly move its featherless body, and its mother needs to sit on it to keep it warm. She chews and swallows crunchy seeds, then **regurgitates** them right into her baby's beak. As the days go by, the little chick grows stronger. It grows fluffy feathers, and within four weeks, the chick is as big as its mother. As an adult, the bird has babies of its own. Eventually, like all living things, the parakeet dies.

Words to Know

regurgitate: to throw up partially digested food to feed a baby.

oxygen: a gas you breathe to live.

Thanks, Sun!

Without the sun, life on Earth couldn't exist. The sun is the source of most of the energy on Earth. It provides the planet's warmth and makes life possible. Plants need sunlight to grow. Without the sun, there would be no plants.

Without plants, the connected circle of life would wither and die. All land animals depend on plants for survival. You depend on plants, too. Plants provide food and **oxygen**.

Living things even need nonliving things to stay alive. Nonliving things include air, rocks, soil, and water. Every part of an ecosystem is like part of a team. Each player interacts with all the other players in the environment. Team Nature keeps the whole system balanced and thriving.

Parakeets Adapting

The parakeet is a small, brightly colored parrot native to warm areas in South America. But wild parakeets live in the streets of New York City and Chicago. How did they come to live in these northern cities? Scientists believe that in 1967, a shipment of birds from South America escaped from New York's Kennedy Airport. They reproduced and thrived. Chicago's parakeets likely escaped from houses and pet shops.

Food Chains and Food Webs

An ecosystem passes the sun's energy along to every member of its team. Microorganisms, plants, and animals mingle. Through **food chains**, they maintain a complex circle of life. All food chains, or flows of energy in ecosystems, begin with plants.

Plants are **producers**. They make their own food. Since food chains start with producers, plants are critical. They form the foundation of the food chain. Plants capture the sun's energy and pass it along to the animals that eat them.

Unlike plants, animals can't produce their own food. Animals are **consumers**, the next links in the chain. They are grouped depending on what they eat.

Words to Know

food chain: a community of animals and plants where each is eaten by another higher up in the chain. Food chains combine into food webs.

producer: an organism that makes its own food.

consumer: an organism that eats other organisms.

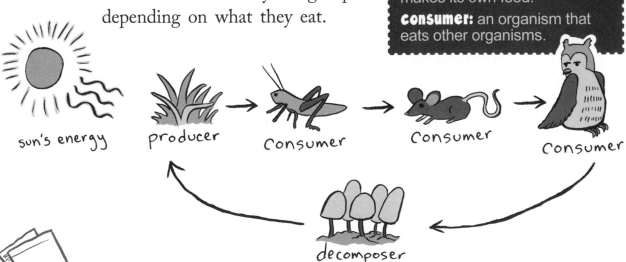

sun's energy   producer   consumer   consumer   consumer

decomposer

The fight for survival means eat or be eaten! Some animals, like the North American elk and the snowshoe hare, gobble plants. These **herbivores** eat crunchy nuts and seeds, nibble fruits and flowers, and chomp on leaves and stems.

Carnivores, such as the great white shark and the great horned owl, are **predators** that eat other animals. Torpedo-shaped with cavernous jaws, great whites ambush their **prey**. They gorge on sea lions, small whales, and other sharks. Great horned owls are sneaky night hunters snacking on shrews, meadow voles, and raccoons. They devour other birds, including ducks and geese.

But **omnivores** aren't fussy! These animals, like cockroaches and wild pond turtles, eat both plants and animals. Are you an omnivore?

Words to Know

herbivore: an animal that eats only plants.

carnivore: an animal that eats only other animals.

predator: an animal that hunts another animal for food.

prey: an animal hunted and eaten by other animals.

omnivore: an animal that eats both plants and animals.

decomposers: organisms such as ants, fungi, and worms that break down wastes, dead plants, and dead animals.

fungi: molds, mushrooms, mildew, and rust. Singular is fungus.

nutrient: a substance an organism needs to live and grow.

fertile: describes soil that is good for growing crops.

Decomposers Are Rottin'

The circle of life includes death. Because of this **decomposers** are a vital link in the food chain. Decomposers include ants, worms, and **fungi**. They do an ecosystem's dirty work, breaking down dead plants and animals so they rot. Decomposers decay chunks of dead wood. They even feast on animal wastes. They're nature's recyclers because they pass **nutrients** back into the soil to keep it **fertile**. Fertile soil means plants can flourish and keep the food chain going. The circle of life rolls on and on.

Chapter 2

Cells Alive!

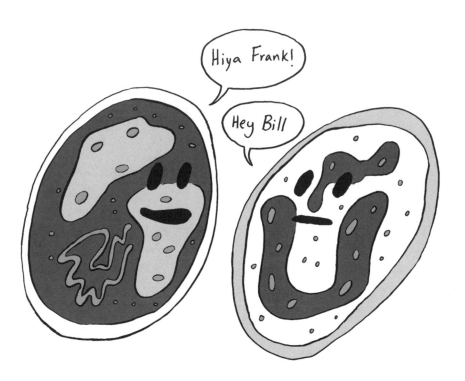

Cells keep living organisms the way they are—alive. Cells are living things. They are the basic, smallest units of all life. A unit is a single part from which larger things are made. Every living thing is made of cells. From **microscopic bacteria** and **amoeba** wriggling in pond scum to a ravenous gator cruising a swamp. From a Venus Flytrap to the frog it snares. From a snow leopard to the mossy branch it snoozes on. And you!

That's why cells are called life's building blocks.

Have you looked at slides through a microscope? Most cells are so teeny you need a microscope to see them. Lenses inside microscopes magnify cells so they appear much larger than they really are. With enlarged images, it's easier to study cells.

One-Celled Wonders

Some organisms, such as the amoeba, are made of only one cell. Single-cell life forms are called **unicellular**. They are smaller in size and simpler than living things made of many cells. You can't see them with the **naked eye**. Where do amoebae live? They're in puddles you leap over, and in mucky soil that squishes under your sneakers. Jelly-like amoebae thrive inside some animals. They supply nibbles of food for water fleas and mussels. When they invade people's bodies, some amoebae can cause harmful illnesses.

Amoebae don't have any hard parts. Made of a glob of colorless liquid called **protoplasm**, these one-celled wonders constantly change shape to eat and move.

Words to Know

microscopic: something so small it can only be seen under a microscope.

bacteria: single-celled organisms found in soil, water, plants, and animals. They help decay food and some bacteria are harmful. Singular is bacterium.

amoeba: a bloblike single-celled organism. Plural is amoebae.

unicellular: made of only one cell.

naked eye: the human eye without help from a microscope.

protoplasm: the colorless liquid that forms the living matter of a cell.

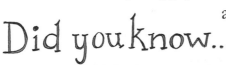

One is all you need, baby.

Did you know...

Have you ridden a unicycle? Read a unicorn tale? The prefix uni- means "one." Are you multitalented? Have you watched movies at a multiplex? Multi- means "more than one."

How can a microscopic blob of jelly get around? With a **pseudopod**, or "false foot." A slimy amoeba forms flowing foot-like bulges from **cytoplasm**. With pseudopods, the amoeba can drag itself to a different location.

Words to Know

pseudopod: a foot-like bulge an amoeba uses to move.

cytoplasm: the gel-like inside of a cell.

fission: the splitting of a single-celled organism into two parts.

asexual: reproduction without male and female cells joining.

Make your own amoeba and feed it! Fill a clear glass halfway with water. That represents a puddle. Add a teaspoon of oil. What shapes form? With a cotton swab, blend the shapes to create one blobby amoeba. Drop an apple or orange seed into the water. That's the prey. Stretch out pseudopods with the swab to surround and capture the prey.

Imagine an amoeba floating in pond scum. A yummy bacterium floats close by. The amoeba oozes toward its lunch. It stretches out pseudopods and surrounds its prey. The single-celled amoeba hauls itself around the organism. Once the bacterium is snared, the amoeba swallows it up and absorbs it into the cytoplasm.

Divide to Multiply

Cells reproduce. They make new cells. When old cells die, new cells replace them. An amoeba reproduces in a process called **fission**. It's an **asexual** process. To reproduce, an amoeba stops moving and splits into two equal parts. It makes an identical copy of itself, and the copy grows into a new organism.

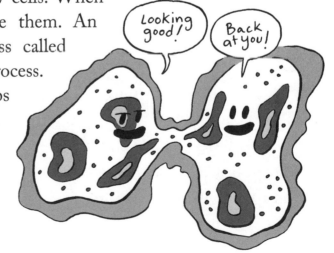

Did you know...

It only takes a pinkie to count the number of cells in an amoeba. But you'd probably lose count if you tried to count the cells in your own body. It's bursting with about 100 trillion cells!

From a single cell to a complex cardiovascular system

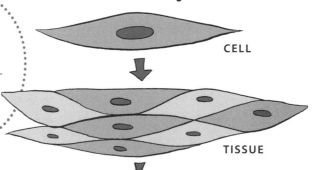

CELL

TISSUE

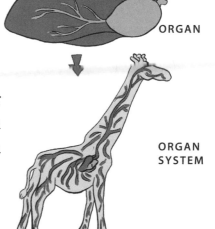

ORGAN

ORGAN SYSTEM

Multicellular Organisms, Get Organized!

Most organisms, including people, other animals, and plants, are made of many cells. They are **multicellular**. These organisms are larger and more complex than unicellular organisms. Multicellular living things contain specialized cells that work together to do a job. Red blood cells carry oxygen through the body. Other cells might be specific to the heart.

Specialized cells form **tissues**, **organs**, and organ systems that function together. How does this system of organization happen? Cells of the same type cluster to form tissues. These tissues group together to create organs. Two or more different organs form an organ system.

Words to Know

multicelluar: made up of many cells.

tissue: a large number of cells similar in form and function that are grouped together.

organ: a body part that has a certain function, such as the heart or kidneys.

Cells Have a Job to Do

Earth's living things are incredibly diverse. Yet cells behave in ways that are similar in all organisms. Each cell has a specific job to perform, and all cells must work together to keep you alive and healthy.

It's hard to imagine that tiny cells have even tinier parts. These **organelles**, or "little organs," carry out certain functions. They all pitch in to tend to the cell's needs. Organelles help the cell take in air and food. They kick out wastes. These teeny organs have huge jobs to tackle.

What jobs? Big boss, shape supporter, food changer, and gatekeeper.

Although plant and animal cells are different, they have some organelles in common. Both contain a large, round **nucleus**. The nucleus is the big boss, like the cell's control tower or brain. The nucleus gives orders to the cell. It tells the cell when to grow and when to reproduce, for example.

Cells are filled with rubbery, sticky cytoplasm. Cytoplasm provides the cell with shape and holds organelles in a gooey grip. Inside the cytoplasm, tube-shaped **mitochondria** are in charge of changing food into energy. Other organelles, including **ribosomes**, **Golgi bodies**, and **endoplasmic reticulum** are also hard at work, while **lysosomes** in animal cells work to break down and digest food.

Words to Know

organelle: a structure inside a cell that performs a special function or job.

nucleus: the central part of a cell.

mitochondria: the parts of the cell that change food into energy.

ribosomes: the protein builders of a cell.

Golgi bodies: sacs that receive proteins from the cell, put them together with other proteins, and send them around the cell.

endoplasmic reticulum: a network of membranes that makes changes and transports materials through the cell.

lysosome: an organelle that aids in digestion.

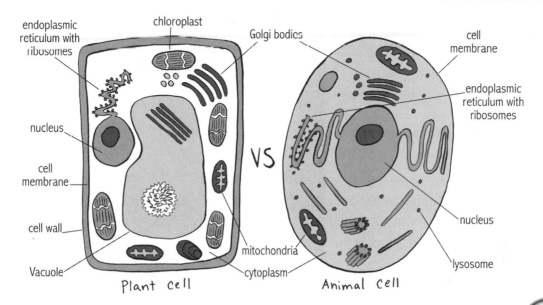

endoplasmic reticulum with ribosomes

chloroplast

Golgi bodies

cell membrane

nucleus

cell membrane

cell wall

Vacuole

mitochondria

cytoplasm

endoplasmic reticulum with ribosomes

nucleus

lysosome

VS

Plant Cell

Animal Cell

A **membrane** surrounds a cell in a layer like a teeny ziplock bag. In a plant cell, membranes are inside a rigid **cell wall** that gives shape to cells. In an animal cell, the membrane is stretchy. In both, the membrane is the gatekeeper. It allows nutrients in and lets wastes out.

Words to Know

membrane: the outer layer of a cell that allows materials to pass in and out.

cell wall: the part of a plant cell that gives shape to the cell.

chloroplasts: the parts of a plant cell in which sunlight is converted to energy.

pigment: a substance that gives something its color.

chlorophyll: the chemical in a plant's cell that gives a plant its green color.

vacuole: a compartment in the cytoplasm of a plant cell that stores food and waste.

How Are Plant Cells Different?

Most green plants are food factories. They produce their own food. Special cells get the job done. **Chloroplasts** are in charge of converting the sun's energy into stored energy. Chloroplasts contain a green **pigment** called **chlorophyll**. Chlorophyll does more than provide plants with a beautiful green color. It also works as a microscopic solar panel that snags the sunlight needed to churn out food. All plant cells contain a **vacuole**. A bag of fluid floating in cytoplasm, the vacuole is the cell's warehouse. It stores pigment, food, and wastes.

EDIBLE CELL MODEL

Kiwi, tangerines, cranberries, and more represent an animal cell's organelles in this project. Light-colored gelatin allows organelles to stand out so you can easily see them! When the gelatin sets, spoon up a jiggly treat!

Be Careful: Make sure to wash your hands before handling food items, and ask an adult to help you with boiling water.

1 Use the mixing bowl, measuring cup, and wooden spoon. Follow the directions on the gelatin package to prepare the mix, but use **only half** the amounts of boiling and cold water indicated on the package. Using less water creates a firmer base for the edible organelles.

2 Allow the gelatin to cool to room temperature. Carefully place the empty ziplock bag inside the saucepan. Ask an adult to help you pour the cooled gelatin, which represents the cytoplasm, into the bag. Fill the bag about one-third full.

Try It!

Do some research to learn about other organelles. Then assign titles that describe the functions they perform in a cell.

3 You're ready to add organelles. Arrange the fruit to represent the nucleus, mitochondria, lysosomes, ribosomes. Add ribbon candy to represent Golgi bodies. Press the ends of the fruit strips together to form a single long strip. Fold it back and forth in a fanned fashion to resemble wavy endoplasmic reticulum.

4 Carefully squeeze the air out of the bag and tightly seal it. Lay the bag flat on the cookie sheet. Gently move the fruit around so the organelles are not bunched together.

5 Place the cookie sheet in the refrigerator so the gelatin can set. Wait at least an hour, then check periodically. Gently touch the bag to check progress. The gelatin may take a few hours to set firmly.

Supplies

- mixing bowl
- measuring cup
- wooden spoon
- box of light-colored gelatin dessert mix (for cytoplasm)
- boiling water
- cold water
- saucepan
- large ziplock storage bag (for cell membrane)
- 1 plum (for nucleus)
- 4 tangerine slices (for mitochondria)
- 4 blueberries (for lysosomes)
- 4 raspberries (for ribosomes)
- 1 piece of hard ribbon candy (for Golgi bodies)
- 4 pieces of fruit strips (for endoplasmic reticulum)
- cookie sheet
- refrigerator
- science journal and pencil
- dish and spoon

6 When the gelatin has set, remove the cookie sheet from the refrigerator. Create a scientific method worksheet in your science journal. Sketch a diagram of the cell and label each of the components.

7 Carefully squeeze the cell into a dish. Dig in and enjoy!

Try It!

Extend the activity by creating a non-edible gelatin model. Replace edible items with those found in nature. Use pinecones, seashells, acorns, and other things you gather outside to represent organelles.

BAGS O' BREAD MOLD

Fungi lack chlorophyll, so they can't obtain energy from the sun and can't produce their own food. To get energy, many fungi feast on dead organisms. Mold is a fuzzy, multicellular fungus that flourishes in many environments. It reproduces with **spores**. You can grow your own mold on slices of bread. What happens when you place them in different environments?

Caution: Some people are allergic to mold spores. Inhaling spores can be harmful. Keep ziplock bags tightly sealed at all times. Don't touch mold. Ask an adult to help you choose environments out of reach of family members and pets. When you finish the project, ask an adult to safely dispose of the sealed bags.

Words to Know

spore: a structure produced by fungi that sprouts and grows into a new fungus.

1 Label the sandwich bags. Write "Bright" on one and "Dark" on the other. Jot the date on each.

2 Rub cotton swabs against a floorboard, a table leg, or another dusty surface to collect samples. Be sure to rub both swabs in the same location. Then, brush one dusty swab over the surface of one slice of bread. Brush the second swab on the other slice.

3 Fill the dropper with water. Drip 5 drops of water onto each slice of bread. Place one slice into the Bright sandwich bag and the other into the Dark bag. Seal the bags tightly.

Did you know...

Grains used to bake breads come from living things.

4 Choose a brightly lit, warm location for the Bright bag such as a sunny windowsill. Choose a cool, dark location for the Dark bag, such as a basement. Let mold spores incubate for a full week.

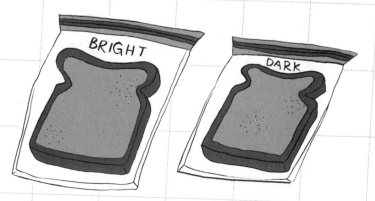

5 Make a scientific method worksheet in your science journal. What do you think will happen to the bread after a week? Which location is better for mold to flourish? Jot down your predictions.

6 After the first two days, gather the bags. Use the magnifying glass to examine samples. Do you observe any mold, or is it still invisible? Note observations on your scientific method worksheet. Sketch and color illustrations of the two samples. Then return the bags to their locations.

7 After five more days, gather the bags. Use the magnifying glass to examine your mold colonies. What do the samples look like now? Jot down observations, and make colored sketches. How do the samples compare? Were your predictions accurate?

Supplies

- permanent marker
- 2 ziplock sandwich bags
- 2 cotton swabs
- 2 slices of bread, or 2 hamburger buns or dinner rolls
- eye dropper
- ¼ cup of water
- science journal and pencil
- magnifying glass
- crayons, markers, or colored pencils

Did you know...

Molds grow in a variety of colors, from bright fluorescent purple to drab olive green and rusty brown. Can you research the different color types of mold and make a chart?

IT'S ALIVE!
YEAST BALLOON BLOW UP

Yeast is a single-celled fungus. Shake a few grains into your palm, and check it out. It may not seem to be alive but it's just **dormant** right now. But watch what happens when you activate a yeast culture. Can you inflate a balloon with it?

Hint: Don't use hot water. That will kill the yeast.

1 Pour baker's yeast into the bottle. Carefully pour warm water into the bottle until it's about one-quarter full. Swirl the bottle in a circular motion to dissolve the yeast. As yeast is absorbed in water, it becomes active. Yeast cells are microscopic, so you won't be able to see any signs of life.

Words to Know

dormant: not growing and developing.

colony: a group of plants or animals living cooperatively together.

Just for Fun

Q: What's the difference between the shining sun and a loaf of bread?

A: One rises from the east, and the other rises from yeast.

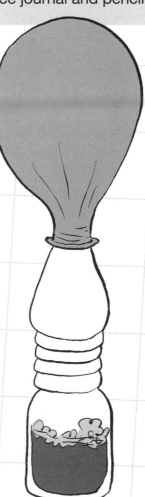

2 Add sugar to the bottle. You're feeding the yeast. Yeast uses sugar's energy to become more active. Swirl the bottle again to dissolve the sugar. How is the yeast changing? Is it bubbly or foamy?

3 Fill the bottle with more of the very warm water. Add water all the way to the top of the neck.

4 Stretch the balloon to loosen it. Blow it up several times. Check to make sure there are no leaks, and then deflate it. Slip the deflated balloon over the bottle's neck.

5 Make a scientific method worksheet to record your predictions and results. Then incubate your yeast culture in a warm location away from drafts. After a few hours, check your experiment. It may take longer, depending on your environment.

What's happening?

As yeast gobbles sugar, it releases CO_2, the gas carbon dioxide. It releases more and more gas, which bubbles into the bottle. Yeast also makes more yeast. As whole **colony** produces more and more gas, the gas has to go somewhere.

Supplies

- package of active dry baker's yeast
- empty plastic water or soda bottle
- very warm tap water, about 110 degrees Fahrenheit (43 degrees Celsius)
- 2 tablespoons sugar
- small balloon
- science journal and pencil

23

Chapter 3

Microbiology Reveals an Invisible World

Did you know that you are an ecosystem for life forms that you can't even see? Wherever you go, an invisible world goes with you. Trillions of microorganisms, some good and some bad, hitch a ride on and inside your body. To microorganisms, your scalp is a thick jungle in which to roam, and one eyelash a towering tree on which to perch. The tip of your fingernail is an exciting cliff.

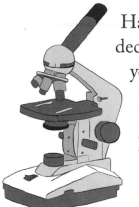

Harmful microorganisms squirm behind your teeth and cause decay. Helpful microorganisms squiggle in your gut to help you digest food. They churn lunch into nutrients, which your cells use for growth and fuel. Most of your body's invisible inhabitants are bacteria, one of Earth's smallest life forms.

MODERN LIGHT MICROSCOPE

With today's technology, you can view microorganisms under light microscopes. Light passes through a slide. As you peer into an eyepiece, the scope displays a magnified image of a **specimen** right under your eye!

HOOKE'S MICROSCOPE

Microscopes reveal an unknown world. But it wasn't until the 1600s that scientists became aware of microscopic cells. As scientists often build on the discoveries of other scientists, Robert Hooke's first microscopes inspired Antoni van Leeuwenhoek toward an explosion of curiosity and discovery. Together, these two **revolutionized** biology.

Words to Know

specimen: a sample of something.

revolutionize: to transform, or make a huge and complete change.

dust mite: a microscopic insect that feeds on dead skin cells. Dust mites are a common cause of allergies.

Did you know...

What's bouncing in the dust bunnies under your bed? It's mostly flakes of your own skin! Your skin's top layer is comprised of dead cells. Every day, some of these dead cells flake off your body and flutter to the floor where they mingle with dust, form a tumbleweed, and roll around. These dead cells provide an all-you-can-eat feast for invisible **dust mites**. Delicious.

Hooked on Cells

Whether belonging to an amoeba, a flea, or a great white shark, most cells are microscopic. Until the invention of microscopes, no scientists had observed cells. No one knew they existed. Microscopes brought these tiny living things into focus. Scopes allowed the discovery of cells. And more.

HOOKE'S DRAWING OF CORK CELLS

In 1665, Robert Hooke (1635–1703), a brilliant English scientist, discovered plant cells. As a boy, Hooke loved machines. He tinkered with clocks and fiddled with mechanical toys. As an adult, Hooke became a scientist. He used his tinkering skills to build **crude** microscopes. In what turned out to be one of his most important discoveries, Hooke sliced a sliver of bark from a cork oak tree. He placed his sample under his homemade scope and was surprised to see rows and rows of tiny boxes. He wrote that these boxes looked like a bee's honeycomb. He called the boxes cells, since they reminded him of little rooms. Without realizing it, Hooke was describing the cell walls of the bark.

HOOKE'S DRAWING OF FLY EYEBALLS

Under his microscope's lens, Hooke viewed molds and **mosses**, **crystals** and **minerals**, and plants and insects. He published his observations in the book *Micrographia*. As the first book to describe microscopic life, *Micrographia* revolutionized science. The book contained incredible, close-up illustrations of his observations. People poured over Hooke's intricate drawings. They marveled at delicate snow crystals, googly fly eyeballs, and spiky barbs on bee stingers.

Words to Know

crude: very basic.

moss: a small seedless plant that grows in soft feathery patches in moist places, such as the ground of a thick forest.

crystal: a solid with its **atoms** arranged in a geometric pattern.

atoms: tiny particles of matter that make up everything.

mineral: a solid, nonliving substance found in the earth and in water.

The Father of Microbiology

Robert Hooke's drawings in *Micrographia* inspired Antoni van Leeuwenhoek (1632–1723), a fabric merchant from Holland, to build his own microscopes. He wanted to see some of these things for himself. Leeuwenhoek ground glass and built small, simple, hand-held scopes. With his love of nature, sense of wonder, and endless curiosity, Leeuwenhoek became a **pioneer** in microbiology. He was the first to discover and describe **protozoa** and bacteria.

Leeuwenhoek enjoyed exploring the world outside his door. In 1674, the curious merchant wondered about the lake near his home. During cold months, the lake sparkled with clear water. But Leeuwenhoek noticed that during the heat of summer, the water turned murky green.

Words to Know

pioneer: to be one of the first to discover something new.

protozoa: one-celled microscopic organisms, such as an amoeba, that can divide only while living inside another organism. Singular is protozoon.

Did you know...

Not all bacteria are bad for you. You've probably eaten healthy bacteria, called probiotics, if you've eaten yogurt or sour cream. Probiotics can help you digest food and keep your immune system strong so you can fight germs. Yogurt contains probiotics when it says on the label that it has live and active cultures.

To try to discover what might cause this change in the quality of the water, Leeuwenhoek scooped a slimy sample of the green water into a glass tube. He examined a drop of the liquid under a homemade lens that he held up to his eye. What he saw were hundreds of green flashes squirming and wriggling around!

Leeuwenhoek marveled at these swimming creatures, alive in a miniature world.

LEEUWENHOEK'S MICROSCOPE

He'd uncovered yet another world, a **microbiome**, that no one had ever seen before! He wrote about, "Very many little animalcules" whose movement "in the water was so fast and so random, upwards, downwards, and round in all directions that it was truly wonderful to see." Scientists later renamed his animalcules, calling them microorganisms.

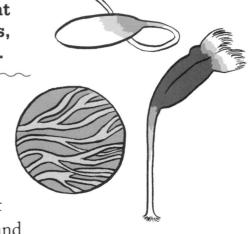

SKETCHES OF ANIMALCULES

Once he made this discovery about the microscopic world living all around us, Leeuwenhoek got curious about what might be living inside of us. He dove into the mouths of two older men who had never cleaned their teeth in their entire lives. After bravely scraping off **plaque** samples, he put them under a microscope.

Words to Know

microbiome: a tiny **biome**.

biome: a natural area with a distinct **climate**, and with plants and animals adapted for life there. Deserts and rainforests are examples of biomes.

climate: average weather patterns in an area over many years.

plaque: a sticky substance that forms on teeth and gums and causes decay.

Planet Protector

Are you taking your explorations on the road to a county, state, or national park? Check with a ranger for permission before you collect samples. Be aware that it might be against the law to do so.

Did you know...

Today's electron microscopes magnify cells two million times using a beam of **electrons** that light specimens for viewing.

What did the specimens reveal? He saw "an unbelievably great company of living animalcules." He said they were "a-swimming more nimbly than any I had ever seen up to this time . . ." Before Leeuwenhoek's discoveries, no one had imagined that there were billions and billions of tiny creatures living right under (and even in!) our noses.

Leeuwenhoek also discovered blood cells and was the first person to view living sperm cells from animals.

Words to Know

electron: a particle in an atom with a negative charge.

sperm: the cell that comes from a male in the reproductive process.

Did you know...

Although Leeuwenhoek built hundreds of scopes during his life, only eight survive today. Many were made of precious gold. After Leeuwenhoek's death, his golden creations were auctioned off by weight.

NOW YOU DON'T SEE IT, NOW YOU DO!

Spores are one-celled structures produced by fungi, which develop into new fungi. Mushrooms are umbrella-shaped fungi. You can make invisible mushroom spores visible!

Caution: It's tricky to tell which wild mushrooms are safe and which are **toxic**. Instead of foraging for wild mushrooms, buy them from a farmer's market or grocery store.

Words to Know

toxic: poisonous.

gills: the part of a mushroom that contains spores.

1 Flip a mushroom upside down. Pop off the stalk beneath the cap if there is one.

PORTOBELLO MUSHROOM

2 Investigate what's under the cap. Does the mushroom have thin, papery **gills** that run under the cap toward the stem? Does it have lots of tiny holes called pores? Or does it have long, thin "teeth" that hang down? These are all different structures that mushrooms have to spread their spores so more mushrooms can grow. If you have a mushroom with gills, run your fingertips over the gills. You should see a brownish powder come out. That powder contains microscopic spores.

3 At the center of the paper or card, position the mushroom with its underside down. Carefully place the bowl over it. Leave the mushroom on the paper for 24 hours.

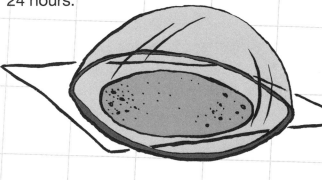

Did you know...

Another meaning of mushroom is "to grow rapidly."

30

4 After 24 hours, carefully lift the bowl. Slip the mushroom off the paper. You should discover a visible spore print.

5 Hold the hairspray about 12 inches above the paper (30 centimeters). Spray a thin layer over the print to lock the spores in place.

6 Use glue to mount your print on a sheet of scrapbook or construction paper. Try this with all the mushrooms you have to see what different prints they make.

Supplies

- different types of mushrooms, such as portobello, shitake, white button (with dark gills), oyster, porcini, hedgehog, chanterelle, and morel
- small sheets of paper or unlined index cards
- glass bowl
- hairspray
- glue
- scrapbook or construction paper

Did you know...

The eerie jack-o-lantern mushroom glows in the dark! Waste products in the gills cause a freaky greenish light.

Nature Detective

Fungi are important decomposers. For energy, fungi feast on dead plants, dead animals, and poop. Fungi suck away water and nutrients from dead organisms, causing them to rot. Mushrooms love cool, dark, moist environments. They grow quickly in clumps and even sprout overnight. After a heavy rainfall, scout outdoors for mushrooms. Search under logs, around tree stumps, and in mounds of decomposing leaves. Sketch what you discover, or snap photos. Use online and library resources to identify different fungi. Remember, some wild mushrooms are poisonous, so don't touch or taste any! Even touching some might result in skin irritations.

GROW MICROBES IN A WINOGRADSKY COLUMN

You can't see microorganisms, but they are alive. Microorganisms need energy, water, and nutrients to thrive. Give them what they need! Build a Winogradsky column, an environment for microorganisms to grow. Use sunlight, newspaper, an egg yolk, and mucky soil to grow microbes in a bottle.

Be Careful: Ask an adult to help cut off the top of the bottle.

1 Choose a place where you can find mucky soil or sand. A combination of mud and sand works well. You might select a freshwater pond or an ocean shore, your own garden, or a forest.

2 Put on the gloves. Use the trowel to scoop out muck. Drop at least 5 cups into one of the small buckets (about 1 liter). Pluck out rocks, twigs, shells, or leaves from the sample. Scoop about 5 cups of water (1 liter) from the same site and drop it into the other small bucket.

3 Have an adult cut off the top third of the bottle to form a column. Set aside the top section to use as a funnel later.

4 Slowly add some water to the muck and stir with the paint stirrer as you pour. Stir until the mixture reaches the consistency of thick cream. You don't want the mixture to be too watery, but make sure it remains fluid and moves freely. You'll need to pour it through the funnel later.

5 Shred a piece of newspaper into tiny pieces and stir them into the mixture.

6 With the sharpener, grind the chalk. Measure out 1 tablespoon of powdered chalk, and stir it into the mixture.

7 Place the egg yolk in a cup and crush it up with the fork. Add the yolk to the mixture.

Supplies

- garden gloves
- garden trowel or small shovel
- 2 small buckets
- measuring cup
- 5 cups of mucky mud/ sand from a garden, forest, pond, lakeshore, or ocean shore (1 liter)
- 5 cups of water from the field site where you obtain the muck (1 liter)
- 2-liter bottle with label removed (clear, to allow in light)
- scissors
- paint stirrer
- newspaper
- pencil sharpener
- piece of chalk (to fit in pencil sharpener)
- measuring spoons
- hard-boiled egg yolk
- cup
- fork
- duct tape
- plastic wrap
- rubber band
- science journal and pencil

continues on next page . . .

8 Fit the funnel into the top of the column. Use the duct tape to secure it in place. Use the measuring spoons to scoop a small amount of the mixture into the funnel. With one hand over the top of the bottle, tap the bottle against the table. You're removing any oxygen inside and allowing the mixture to settle.

9 Repeat the process of adding small amounts of the mixture and settling it at the bottom of the bottle. Continue until the bottle is almost, but not completely, full.

10 Remove the funnel from the bottle and briskly stir the mixture. This removes air bubbles. Allow the bottle to sit undisturbed. After half an hour, make sure the water that settled at the top of the bottle is about three-quarters of an inch deep (2 centimeters). If necessary, pour out or add a bit of water.

11 Seal the top of the bottle with plastic wrap. Use the rubber band to secure the plastic in place. Put the bottle in a bright location near a window but out of direct sunlight and away from heat. The bottle will stay in this location for four weeks.

12 Leave the bottle in position. Try not to shift it when you return to study its progress over the four-week period. Make a scientific method worksheet to describe your experiment and record your predictions of what changes will occur in the column over time.

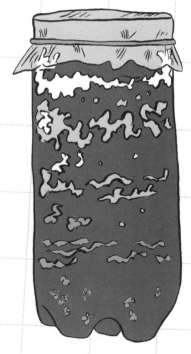

13 For four weeks, check the column the same day each week. Create a colored sketch of your observations each time you study it. You will probably notice purplish and green blotches growing first. They appear at the side of the column facing the sunlight. What other changes do you observe?

What's happening?

Over a period of time, microbes will grow in layers of different colors. They'll create their own ecosystem! Why do layers of microorganisms grow in the column? Oxygen concentration is highest at the top. Microbes that need oxygen grow there, near the surface. Oxygen is lower at the bottom. Microorganisms that don't need much oxygen hang out there.

Planet Protector

Did you find any plastic bags, crushed cans, empty water bottles, or other trash at your field site? Sure, it's annoying. You didn't leave it there. But if you clear away just a few pieces of trash that others left behind, you're making an impact. Little things add up, so please pitch in and pitch it!

Carry a bag for collecting trash at field sites. If you find any bottles and cans, toss them in recycling bins.

COLLECT POND SAMPLES IN YOUR OWN PLANKTON NET

Plankton is the first link in the marine food chain. Plankton are microscopic plants and animals that float at the surface of fresh and salt water. They provide food for other organisms. For example, in a tropical reef ecosystem, damselfish and fusiliers nibble plankton.

Make your own plankton net to collect samples. Will you discover "animalcules, a-swimming nimbly" when you view samples under a scope like Leeuwenhoek? Make a scientific method worksheet in your science journal to organize your experiment. Try to borrow a microscope if you don't have one.

Be Careful: Wear the life jacket, and always use caution around water. Ask an adult to help you collect samples. If you are boating on a lake, river, or ocean, slow way down and drag the net in the water behind you for a minute or two. Ask an adult to help you with the needle and thread.

· ·

1 To make the net, bend the wire to form a circle. Secure the ends with duct tape. Roll the "thigh" end of the tights over the wire circle. Use heavy thread or fishing line to sew it around the wire.

2 Cut off the foot of the tights if there is one. Slip the "ankle" end over the mouth of the jar or bottle. Wind string or fishing line around the top, and tie it securely. Reinforce the tied area with duct tape.

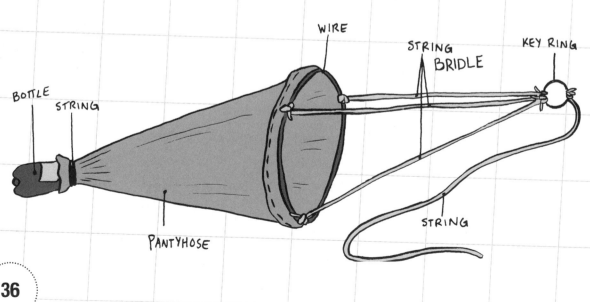

WIRE

STRING
BRIDLE

KEY RING

BOTTLE
STRING

PANTYHOSE

STRING

3 Make the bridle to tow the net. Cut three, 20-inch lengths of string (50 centimeters). Securely tie them at three equal spaces around the circle. Draw the three loose ends through the key ring. Tie them tightly to form the bridle's ring.

4 Cut a fourth length of string and tie it to the bridal ring so you can tow it for plankton samples. Find a safe location on a sturdy dock or pier. Put on the life jacket. Slowly walk up and down the dock towing the net through the water to scoop samples into the bottle.

5 Back indoors, use the eye dropper to place drops of your water sample on a slide. Examine the plankton under a microscope. Sketch the microorganisms you observe on your scientific method worksheet, and jot down descriptions. Conduct research to identify and label them.

plankton found!!

Supplies

- science journal and pencil
- 20 inches thin wire (50 centimeters)
- duct tape
- leg cut off of old pantyhose or fine, light-colored tights
- heavy thread
- strong fishing line
- scissors
- needle
- small jar or bottle
- key ring
- life jacket
- eye dropper
- microscope and slides

Words to Know

crustacean: an animal such as a crab or shrimp with a hard outer shell, jointed limbs, and two sets of antennae.

Did you know...

The blue whale, the ocean's largest organism, feasts on one of the ocean's tiniest organisms. Krill are tiny **crustaceans** that resemble shrimp. When feeding, a blue whale sucks down 1.5 tons of krill daily. According to the Ocean Alliance, that's like scarfing down the meat from 8,000 quarter-pound burgers!

MICROORGANISMS AND SEED SPEED

There's more to soil than meets the eye. The naked eye, that is. On your mark, get set, GO! Conduct a seed speed sprint to discover if seeds sprout when there are no microorganisms in the soil.

Be Careful: Ask an adult to help you with the oven, and don't forget to use oven mitts!

1 Create a scientific method worksheet in your science journal to make predictions and record your observations. Then go outside to locate fertile soil in your garden or a nature area. You'll know soil is fertile if plants are growing in it.

2 Put on gloves. Carefully brush away leaf litter to reveal the soil. Use the trowel and spoons to dig down about 2 inches (5 centimeters). Place a soil sample on the plate. You'll want several large spoonfuls, to fill each jar halfway or more.

3 Lightly sift the sample and spread it out with your fingertips. Examine it with the lens. What do you see?

4 If you've unearthed critters such as roly-poly pill bugs and worms, gently return them to the hole. Seal the rest of the sample in the ziplock bag.

5 Indoors, preheat the oven to 180 degrees Fahrenheit (82 degrees Celsius). Prepare two sticky notes, labeled "Uncooked Sample" and "Cooked Sample." Place one label on each jar.

6 Divide the soil into two equal parts. Pour one into the "Uncooked Sample" jar for now. Set it aside. Pour the second into the pie pan.

Did you know...

In one fistful of soil, you'll unearth hundreds or even thousands of different kinds of microorganisms!

Supplies

- science journal and pencil
- garden gloves
- garden trowel
- old spoons
- paper plate
- magnifying lens
- ziplock bag
- oven
- sticky notes
- permanent marker
- 2 jars of equal size
- pie pan
- oven mitts
- bean seeds
- water

7 Place the pie pan in the oven for 20 minutes to kill any microorganisms. With an adult's help, remove the sample from the oven and allow it to thoroughly cool.

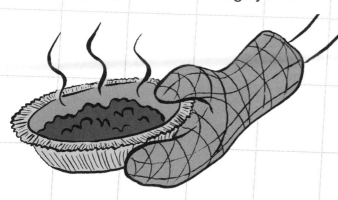

8 As the soil cools, divide the bean seeds into two equal groups. Plant one group in the "Uncooked Sample" jar. When the cooked sample cools, carefully place it in the "Cooked Sample" jar. Plant the second group of seeds in it.

Planet Protector

When you collect soil samples, please take no more than you need. Afterward, smooth over areas where you dug.

continues on next page . . .

39

activity

9 Lightly water each jar of seeds. Select a warm, sunny location for growth. For 10 days, provide the same amount of sunlight and water for each. Predict which sample will grow faster. Will microorganisms in soil help or hurt seeds?

Nature Detective

Dig it! You're looking below the leaf litter to dig at a shallow depth, at soil's ground level. In this **topsoil**, soil is composed of silt, sand, clay, and organic matter. Organic matter is decaying plants and animals. Depending on where you live and recent weather conditions, you might unearth water, too. You may discover rocks. Why is the leaf litter thick in some places and thinner in others? Is the soil different in these places too? Draw in your science journal to illustrate what your soil sample looks like. Can you identify the different components? Do you find more organisms in the soil under a thick layer of leaf littler or under a thinner layer? Why?

Words to Know

topsoil: the top layer of soil.

Chapter 4

Plants Make Life Possible

Earth's plants boast remarkable diversity. Patchy **lichens** are adapted for super-short Arctic growing seasons, while prickly pear cactuses are able to resist withering in harsh deserts. **Algae** mostly exist in the water, while towering redwood trees stretch tall towards the sky.

Words to Know

lichen: yellow, green, and gray plants that grow in patches on rocks. Lichen are made of algae and fungi.

algae: plants that live mainly in water. They do not have leaves, roots, or stems.

Plants were the first organisms adapted to life on land. On land, plants can capture more intense sunlight to perform food-making wonders.

Plants Are Living Things

Imagine a meadow in late summer. A weeping willow tree spreads out like an umbrella. It sways gently in the breeze. Sleek green leaves tickle clumps of yellow carpet moss at your feet. Fern fronds sway. Wood violets with bright purple flowers peek over heart-shaped leaves. Bristly burrs crackle under your sneakers. Inside are sweet beechnut kernels, a favorite food of deer and wild turkeys. Blue jays squabble over juicy black currants. Rabbits nibble tasty clover.

Plants in the meadow, like plants everywhere on Earth, make life possible. All animals depend on them for survival.

Plants provide the food we eat and the oxygen we breathe. Without plants, Earth's **atmosphere** couldn't support life. Sometimes we forget plants are living things. Maybe it's because we don't see them moving in front of us the way we see animals constantly in motion. But what about that glorious moment when flower buds burst open to welcome spring? And what about the nutritious vegetables that grow from the plants you've nurtured in your garden? The movement is so slow we can't watch it happen.

But plants are alive, and they're running their own food factories. In fact, thousands of chemical reactions and processes are taking place every second inside plant cells!

Symbiosis

Lichens are made up of algae and fungi growing in **symbiosis**. This is a relationship between two organisms that rely on each other. It's a win-win partnership that's beneficial for both. How do the algae and fungi in lichens help each other? Algae contain chlorophyll and produce food from the sun's energy. Fungi protect algae. In return, fungi gain nutrients from algae.

Words to Know

atmosphere: the mixture of gases surrounding a planet.

symbiosis: the relationship between two different organisms, in which one or both benefit.

root: the underground plant structure that anchors the plant and takes in water and minerals from soil.

stem: the plant structure that supports leaves, flowers, and fruits.

seed: the part of a plant that holds all the beginnings of a plant.

pollen: a fine, yellow powder produced by flowering plants. Pollen fertilizes the seeds of other plants as it gets spread around by the wind, birds, and insects.

Plant Structure

Plants consist of **roots**, **stems**, and leaves. They grow from **seeds**, and most produce flowers and fruits. Each of these six parts tackles a special job. Flowers are the showy part of a plant that plays an important role in the reproductive process. Their colors and smells attract insects and birds that spread their **pollen**.

A plant's fruits can be sweet and tasty, but they also cover and protect seeds. Seeds create new plants.

Inside a seed is the energy and materials
that a plant needs for growth until it sprouts
its first leaves above the ground.

Roots, stems, and leaves are not reproductive parts. Sprawling underground, hairy roots are the anchors that hold plants in place. Roots suck up water and minerals from the soil. They also store extra food that plants make.

Stems are above-ground supporters and transporters. Sturdy stems prop up plants and hold leaves, flowers, and fruits. Stems also transport water, minerals, and sugar to the roots and leaves of the plant. Leaves are in charge of producing food for the whole plant.

The leaves are the core
of the food factories
where sunlight gets
turned into food through
photosynthesis.

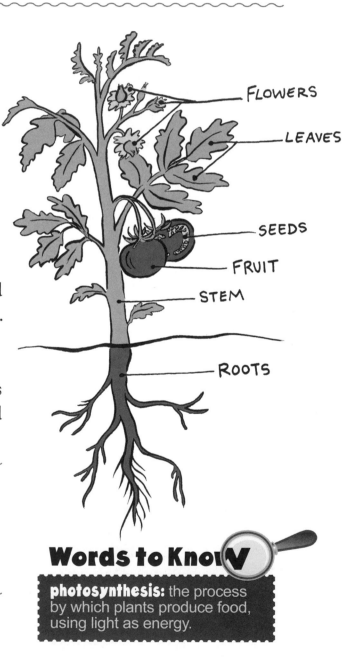

FLOWERS

LEAVES

SEEDS

FRUIT

STEM

ROOTS

Words to Know

photosynthesis: the process
by which plants produce food,
using light as energy.

Photosynthesis: Putting Together with Light

Photosynthesis is the process green plants and some algae use to produce food. Photo means "light." Synthesis means "putting together." Photosynthesis means "putting together with light." So it's not surprising that this amazing process requires sunlight. Plants convert light from the sun into the energy they need to grow. They store the converted energy as **glucose**, which is a simple sugar.

In addition to sunlight, what other ingredients do plants use to whip up food? Water from soil (H_2O), and carbon dioxide from air (CO_2). Above and below ground, plant parts put these ingredients to work.

Photosynthesis mainly takes place in leaves. In leaf cells, chloroplasts filled with green chlorophyll snatch the sun's energy.

Words to Know

glucose: the simple sugar that plants produce through photosynthesis.

LIGHT ENERGY

OXYGEN

CARBON DIOXIDE

CHLOROPHYLL

GLUCOSE

WATER

Did you know...

Water, sugar, and minerals move throughout plants. This movement is called translocation. A tissue called xylem carries water and minerals from roots to stems and leaves. Phloem, another tissue, moves the sugary food made in photosynthesis to the parts of the plant that don't make food, such as the roots, where it can be stored.

Thirsty roots sprawling deep into the soil suck up water. The stem moves the water along, all the way to the leaves. **Stomata** dot the outside of leaves. Like mini mouths, these **pores** open and shut, allowing **water vapor** and CO_2 gases to enter and exit the plant. Most land plants contain stomata on the bottom of their leaves and most **aquatic** plants contain them on the top. Chloroplasts turn sunlight, H_2O, and CO_2 into **carbohydrates**, or simple sugars, that are the plant's food.

In the astonishing circle of life, plants don't only feed themselves. As the producers in food chains and food webs, they provide nourishment for animals and people, too.

Words to Know

stomata: tiny pores on the outside of leaves that allow gases and water vapor to pass in and out.

pore: a tiny opening through which substances pass.

water vapor: water as a gas, like steam, mist or fog.

aquatic: living or growing in water.

carbohydrate: the sugar that is the source of food and energy in a plant.

evolve: to gradually develop over time and become more complex.

Did you know...

Some scientists theorize that photosynthesis **evolved** over 3 billion years ago, not long after the first living organism appeared on Earth. Scientists think that before then Earth's atmosphere didn't contain oxygen.

Air Purifiers

Plants keep our air clean! They produce clean oxygen, a gas necessary for animals and people to survive. Plants don't breathe the way we do, but they do take air in and let it out. Animals and people breathe in oxygen and breathe out carbon dioxide. Plants do the reverse.

Through stomata, plants take in carbon dioxide through their leaves. As they breathe in, they also remove toxins and pollutants from the air. Clean oxygen exits the stomata as a waste product. At the same time, in a process called **transpiration**, stomata release water vapor. About 10 percent of the moisture found in the atmosphere comes from plants.

Words to Know

transpiration: the process by which plants give off water vapor and waste products.

sediment: loose rock particles such as sand or clay.

In many plants, there's no gas exchange at night. With no sunlight, stomata shut down the food factory. They take a break from photosynthesizing. Almost like they're dozing!

Did you know...

In 2010, a team of scientists from Ancona, Italy, discovered three new mysterious species in waters near Crete, Greece. The mystery of these species is that they don't need oxygen to breathe! Only a millimeter long, the creatures resemble tiny jellyfish wearing shells. Scientists found them 2.2 miles below the surface (3.5 kilometers), in **sediment** at the floor of the Mediterranean Sea.

47

Beef and Bean Burrito Break Down

People get most of their nutrition from plants. Sometimes you go straight to the source. You snack on a crunchy apple or munch baby carrots. Other times, it's more complicated. Did you know even a yummy beef and bean burrito is linked to plants?

Recipe ingredients are beef, beans, salsa, and flour tortillas. Beef comes from cows, which graze on grasses. Beans are seeds from bean plants. Diced tomatoes and onions make up salsa. Tomatoes grow on vines, and onions are edible bulbs that grow underground. Flour for tortillas is ground from cereal grains, which are small seeds or fruits. Even a dab of guacamole and a sprinkle of olives on the side are linked to plants. Guacamole is made from mashed avocado, which grows on trees. And olives grow on . . . olive trees.

Did you know...

What is the difference between a fruit and a vegetable? A vegetable is a part of a plant that is eaten, such as the leaves (spinach), stems (celery), roots (carrots), and flowers (cauliflower). To **botanists**, a fruit is the ripened part of a plant that develops from the female reproductive part. The fruit is located at the base of a flower. It contains the plant's seed or seeds. Inside fruits, you'll find seeds from flowering plants. So what are tomatoes, avocados, and olives? Fruits or veggies? They're fruits that people typically eat as veggies! Tomatoes are filled with seeds. Avocados and olives contain **pits**.

Words to Know

botanist: a scientist who studies plant life.

pit: the hard seed of a fruit that has only one seed.

Did you know...

People have used plants in medicines since ancient times. Ancient Egyptians and Greeks chewed willow bark to ease headaches and **arthritis** pain. Present-day scientists discovered willow bark holds salicylic acid. Scientists used salicylic acid to create the modern painkiller aspirin.

Bogged Down With Carnivorous Plants

Plants flourish in every environment on the planet. They are adapted to survive in the extreme ecosystems of broiling deserts and frigid Arctic regions.

Scientists believe there are at least 260,000 species of plants on Earth!

Some plants have even evolved as meat-eaters that snare and devour insects. Venus flytraps look like they're from, well, Venus. Depending on where you live, you might be able to find these toothy plants in your own ecosystem. In the wild, they grow in North and South Carolina's **bogs**. These freshwater **wetlands** grow on top of a spongy mat of sphagnum moss, which decays and turns into **peat**.

Peat does not provide the nutrients needed for plants to grow. In this poor soil, Venus flytraps rely on extreme adaptations for survival. They don't suck up minerals from soil through root systems like other plants. Instead, their specialized leaves have evolved to take in nutrients as they feast on flesh.

Words to Know

arthritis: a medical condition that causes swollen joints, stiffness, and pain.

bog: a marshy wetland made of decomposing plants.

wetland: an area where the land is soaked with water, such as a swamp.

peat: waterlogged, decomposed organic matter.

Did you know...

The Venus flytrap is North Carolina's official state carnivorous plant. Unfortunately, the amazing plant is in danger of **extinction** in the wild.

Each flytrap looks like a clam with bristly teeth. Lined with trigger hairs, its leaves hang open like a gaping mouth. Sweet nectar inside lures flies, spiders, bees, and moths. When prey brushes two or more times against the leaves' trigger hairs—snap! The flytrap clamps shut.

The trapdoor stays totally closed while the plant slowly digests its dinner.

It can take the flytrap two weeks to dissolve the soft inside parts of its prey. Then the trapdoor springs open. The crusty outer part of the prey remains in the leaves until wind and rain eventually flush away the crispy carcass.

Try It!

Break it down with plants! Can you link a peanut butter and banana sandwich to plants? Apart from the banana, it doesn't seem very plant-like. Yet, sandwich bread is made from wheat. Wheat is a plant. Peanut butter is ground from the peanut, part of the **legume** and pea family. A plant. Choose a favorite food such as pepperoni pizza, fish tacos, or spaghetti and meatballs. Break down the ingredients and link them to plants.

Words to Know

extinction: when a species dies out and there are no more left in the world.

legume: a plant that has flowers and produces edible seeds, such as nuts, peas, soybeans, and lentils.

Nature Detective

Plants are essential to the food chain. Take a nature walk to view feeding relationships in action. Locate a spot for quiet observation. You can use binoculars to watch far-away living things and zoom in with a magnifying glass to observe others up close. Study tree bark for evidence of gnawing. Do you notice piles of wood chips scattered around tree trunks? That's probably evidence of nature's lumberjacks and engineers at work—beavers! What insects, birds, and animals munch plants? You might spot a deer gnawing tender twigs, sheep grazing on clover, or ducks slurping algae. What critters are eating other animals? Perhaps a hammock spider snared a fly in its sticky web. Or a robin yanked a plump earthworm from the ground. Which species are competing for the same food sources? You might spy a chipmunk sneaking an acorn away from a squirrel's stash. Illustrate a food chain or web in your science journal to record your observations.

Did you know...

To prepare for winter months when food is scarce, busy squirrels hide food. Squirrels dig up garden soil and bury acorns. They stash seeds and nuts under leaf litter and inside tree stumps, even in flowerpots in your own backyard! When it's time to eat, squirrels sniff out the hidden places. Sometimes, the sneaky rodents outsmart themselves and forget where they concealed their treasures. Then what? Buried and scattered seeds create new trees.

NUTRITIOUS AND DELICIOUS PLANT PARTS SALAD

Toss a colorful, nutritious plant salad! Include leaves, flowers, stems, fruits, roots, seeds, and nuts. Harvest ingredients from your home garden if you have one. Or check out a farmer's market or grocery store to round up produce. Challenge yourself to try something new and exciting. How about fresh fennel or jicama? Star fruit or zucchini blossoms?

Be Careful: Ask an adult to help with any chopping, and with any ingredients that require cooking. Make sure all ingredients come from a safe source. Don't eat anything plucked from public places because they might have been sprayed with pesticides.

1 Wash your hands. Then wash each fresh fruit or vegetable, and allow them to drain or dry. If you are using frozen or canned ingredients, prepare them according to the directions. Use the strainer to strain canned beans, for example.

2 Leaves form the bulk of the salad! Ask an adult to help you use the knife and cutting board to chop, shred, or cut the leaves into bite-sized pieces. Place the greens into the large bowl.

3 Slice the flowers and cut the stems for variety and nutrition. Add them to the bowl.

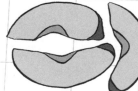

4 Fruits add special zing! Peel fruit as necessary, and remove any pits or seeds. Cut into pieces and add them to the bowl.

5 Time for protein! Add your seeds to the mix (¼ to ½ cup is probably enough or 90 to 180 grams).

6 How about protein with a crunchy texture? Add about ¼ cup nuts (about 25 grams).

7 Toss the salad gently using wooden spoons or tongs to mix all the ingredients. Serve with your favorite dressing.

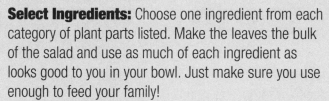

Supplies

- ingredients from the list that follows
- can opener
- strainer
- knife
- cutting board
- large salad bowl
- measuring cups
- wooden spoons or salad tongs
- salad dressing

Select Ingredients: Choose one ingredient from each category of plant parts listed. Make the leaves the bulk of the salad and use as much of each ingredient as looks good to you in your bowl. Just make sure you use enough to feed your family!

- **leaves:** cabbage, kale, lettuce, spinach, turnip greens
- **flowers:** broccoli, cauliflower, nasturtium, squash blossoms, zucchini blossoms
- **stems:** asparagus, bamboo shoot, celery, fennel, Swiss chard
- **fruits:** apple, avocado, orange, star fruit, tomato
- **roots**: beet, carrot, jicama, onion, shallot
- **seeds:** black-eyed peas, edamame, garbanzo beans, pinto beans OR ¼ cup seeds such as sunflower seeds
- **nuts:** slivered almonds, hazelnuts, halved pecans, pine nuts, chopped walnuts

Just for Fun

Q: Why do potatoes make great Nature Detectives?

A: They always keep their eyes peeled!

Nature Detective

Activating the senses is a fantastic way to explore nature. Whenever you make an observation, you use one or more senses. Don't use your sense of taste, though! Many plants you'll encounter outdoors look alike. It's tricky to know which are safe to eat and which are deadly poisonous. Sampling even a tiny bit of the wrong plant can be hazardous. It takes an expert to positively identify edible plants. So play it safe. Don't eat any part of wild plants. Try replacing your sense of taste with your sense of wonder. Ask open-ended questions including I wonder why . . . and I wonder what will happen if . . .

HOW DOES YOUR MYSTERY GREENHOUSE GARDEN GROW?

Collect soil samples from three different field sites to plant in a mini greenhouse. What mysterious sprouts shoot up?

1 Select three sites for collecting samples. You might choose your backyard, a playground, a field, a nature preserve, or a beach. Label each ziplock bag with the marker to identify the site. At each site, wear garden gloves. Use the trowel or shovel to collect soil. Pour the sample into the appropriate bag, and seal it.

2 Use the ruler to measure inside the shoebox lid. Divide the lid into three equal horizontal sections. Draw a line across each section. Line the lid with plastic wrap to make a waterproof bottom for your greenhouse.

3 Make 3 garden stakes with sticky notes and toothpicks. On each sticky note, write the name of one of your field sites. Carefully poke a toothpick through the sticky note to make a little flag. Set the stakes aside for now.

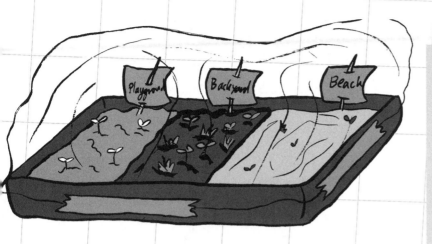

Supplies

- 3 ziplock bags
- permanent marker
- garden gloves
- garden trowel or small shovel
- ruler
- shoebox lid
- plastic wrap
- sticky notes
- toothpicks
- magnifying glass
- science journal and pencil
- water
- tape

4 Pour the first sample into its section of the lid. Use the magnifying glass to examine the sample. What color is it? Is it moist, dry, sandy? Do you see any seeds? Any roots or shoots? Press the identifying toothpick stake into the soil. Repeat with the second and third samples. Start a scientific method worksheet in your science journal. Record your observations and predict what plants will sprout.

5 Lightly water, but don't flood, the samples. With another sheet of plastic wrap, create a puffy roof for the greenhouse and tape it securely in place. Place the greenhouse in a sunny location.

6 How long does it take plants to sprout? Are the plants different or the same among the samples? Can you identify any? Record your observations in your journal.

Did you know...

What are herbivores eating in your field site? You might spot herbivores like Gambel's quail, mourning doves, white-tailed deer, and hares nibbling seeds and nuts. You might observe omnivores like raccoons chomping juicy berries and wild turkeys gobbling tender roots. Yet, those plant parts could still be poisonous to people.

FLOWER POUNDING T-SHIRT

Harvest vibrant flowers at peak bloom, and pound petals to create a printed image on a T-shirt. If you can, use a T-shirt labeled "PFD." That means it's prepared for dying to hold flower colors.

Be Careful: Ask an adult for help with the pruner.

1 Head out to pick and snip your flowers. Choose flowers at peak bloom, when they are rich with color. Flowers that have begun to wilt won't work as well. Harvest flowers early in the day, after the dew has dried but before the sun's heat droops them. Wearing garden gloves, and with an adult's help, snip flowers from the top of the stem. Seal the flowers in plastic containers, and carry the containers in your collection bag.

2 Spread wax paper over a table or other sturdy surface. Place your flowers on the wax paper. Use the pruners to snip away remaining bits of stem. With tweezers, remove everything from inside the flower so you have just the petals. Arrange the petals to create a design you like.

3 Carefully place the front side of the shirt on top of the flower-covered wax paper. Use the rubber mallet to gently pound the shirt over each area of flowers. You are transferring plant pigment to fabric! To prevent smearing, wipe the mallet on a clean rag each time you pound flowers of different colors.

Try It!

Try pounding autumn leaves that aren't brittle, too!

4 Lift the shirt away from the wax paper. Place the T-shirt face-up on the table. Allow the pigment to dry thoroughly. Then, use the fabric marker to carefully outline each flower print.

5 Prepare the dye-set mixture. Combine the salt and water in a plastic tub. Allow the shirt to soak for about 30 minutes. Then hang the shirt up to dry. You'll find that the flower images will fade over time. How can you preserve the pigment? Try turning the shirt inside out when it's time to wash it. Then hand wash and hang dry.

Supplies

- fresh flowers, such as geraniums, hollyhocks, impatiens, pansies, phlox, zinnias
- garden gloves
- pruner or scissors
- several small plastic containers with lids
- collection bag
- wax paper
- tweezers
- white T-shirt
- rubber mallet
- clean rags
- fabric marker
- ½ cup table salt (150 grams)
- 8 cups water (about 2 liters)
- plastic tub

Just for Fun

Q: What did one rose say to the other rose?

A: Hiya, bud!

COOL CHROMATOGRAPHY

What color pops to mind when you think of a leaf? Green, right? But is green the only pigment present? Create leaf rubbings and treat them to reveal their true colors! Create a scientific method worksheet in your science journal to record your predictions and observations.

Caution: Ask an adult for help. Use caution with rubbing alcohol, and work in an area that's well **ventilated**. Alcohol is **flammable**. It should not be splashed into eyes or onto skin and should be properly disposed of when the activity is complete.

Words to Know

ventilate: to supply fresh air into a room or enclosed place.

flammable: something that burns very easily.

coniferous: describes cone-bearing shrubs and trees, often with needles for leaves. Coniferous trees do not lose their leaves each year.

deciduous: describes plants and trees that shed their leaves each year.

1 Wear the lab coat or shirt and goggles. Cut the coffee filter into three strips approximately 1 inch wide (2.5 centimeters) and 4 inches long (10 centimeters). The length of your filter strip may vary according to the height of your jar. They need to be long enough to stick out the top.

2 Turn the leaf from the first plant upside down. Place it on one filter strip, about 1 inch from the bottom (2 centimeters). With the pencil point, rub gently on the leaf. Create a rubbing on the strip about the size of a penny. Reposition the leaf and continue rubbing over the same area to darken the spot on the filter. Repeat with the other two leaves, using a fresh filter strip for each.

3 Ask an adult to fill the jar with ½ inch of alcohol (1 centimeter). Tape the filter strips vertically around the inside of the jar so that the bottom of the strips touch the bottom of the jar.

4 Over time, the alcohol should travel to the tops of the strips. Put on the gloves and remove the strips with tweezers once the alcohol has reached the top.

5 Allow the strips to dry on newspaper. Then study them. What pigments did you reveal? You might notice shades of brown, red, orange, and yellow—fall colors in many areas of North America. Those pigments are always present in leaves. Why can't you always see them? Chlorophyll's lush green shades of spring and summer conceal the others.

Supplies

- science journal and pencil
- large, long-sleeved shirt or lab coat
- safety goggles
- coffee filter
- scissors
- small clear glass jar
- 1 large leaf from each of 3 different plants
- pencil
- rubbing alcohol
- tape
- goggles
- gloves
- tweezers
- newspaper

Nature Detective

Leaves decorate the world in a huge array of shapes, sizes, and shades. Gather a variety of leaves from ferns, mosses, and **coniferous** and **deciduous** trees. Then, use online and print sources to identify their specific plants. *National Audubon Society First Field Guide to Trees* is a fantastic resource in your Nature Detective toolkit. It will help you identify trees and share information on their characteristics and life cycles. You can create wax paper pressings, collages, and wreaths to show off your greenery!

Chapter 5

Plant Life Cycles

Food and fruits. Fibers and fuel. Fields of flowers. These are all ways that plants enrich our lives. They are key to our survival. If we run out of plants, we're all in trouble. But naturally, plants are designed to keep their species alive and thriving.

Just how do plants make more of themselves?

Female and Male Plant Parts

Flowers exist in nearly endless varieties. A flower has one main function: to produce seeds. Most seeds start out tiny. In the right conditions, they flourish and grow to produce new plants.

Flowers can have all male parts or all female parts, but many have a combination of both. The male and female parts make seeds. How? An egg cell from the female part and a germ cell from a grain of pollen in the male part join to become seeds.

The **pistil** is the female, seed-producing organ, usually located right in the middle of the flower. If you touch the top of the pistil, you'll notice a sticky opening. That's the **stigma**. During reproduction, the stigma grabs male pollen grains.

The **style** is a tube shaped like a stalk. The style supports the stigma. At the bottom of the style is a bulgy, pear-shaped **ovary**. The ovary holds eggs, or **ovules**.

Words to Know

pistil: the female, seed-producing reproductive part of a flower. It includes the ovary, style, and stigma.

stigma: the upper part of the pistil, which receives pollen.

style: the stalk-like tube that extends from the ovary to support the stigma.

ovary: the part of the pistil in a flower that bears ovules and ripens into a fruit.

ovule: a small structure that develops into a seed after it joins with a grain of pollen.

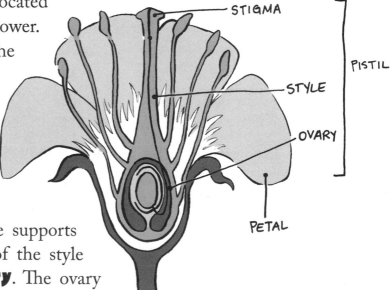

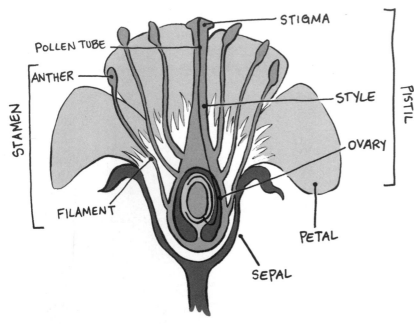

STIGMA

POLLEN TUBE

ANTHER

STAMEN

FILAMENT

STYLE

OVARY

PISTIL

PETAL

SEPAL

Words to Know

stamen: the male, pollen-producing reproductive part of a flower. It includes the filament and anther.

filament: the stalk that supports the anther.

anther: the flower part that produces and holds pollen.

fertilize: to join female and male cells to produce seeds and offspring.

sepals: the special leaves that enclose a flower.

petals: the showy, brightly colored outer area of a flower.

pollinator: an insect or other animal that transfers pollen from the male part of a flower to the female part of a flower.

The **stamen** is a flower's male, pollen-producing organ. Not all flowers contain the same number of stamens, but all stamens have two parts. The **filament** is a thread-like stalk. At the filament's tip, it holds up the **anther**. The anther produces pollen, which is often yellow. This sticky, dusty powder contains male reproductive cells, called germ cells. When the germ cell of a pollen grain joins an egg cell, the egg is **fertilized**. Then the ovary ripens into a fruit and the ovules become the seeds.

Flowering plants also contain **sepals**. These protective leaves are tucked under outer leaves and **petals**. Sepals keep young buds safe until they are ready to show their beautiful flowers. Magenta, apricot, lavender! Have you ever wondered why petals come in such a glitzy bouquet of colors? And an abundance of shapes like trumpets, saucers, and lace? It's because plants are fixed in place. They have to pull out all the stops to attract **pollinators**.

Showy, sweet-scented flowers welcome
pollinators with promises of yummy nectar.
Cushy petals are pillows for the bees and wasps
that hang out to enjoy a leisurely meal.

Welcome, Pollinators!

Plant reproduction depends on **pollination**, when pollen transfers to the stigma. Sometimes one plant's pollen falls directly onto its own stigma. This process is called **self-pollination**. How does pollen from one plant reach another plant's stigma? How does **cross-pollination** happen between plants on opposite ends of a meadow?

Wind and rain scatter pollen. Bees, butterflies, and birds also do the trick. Even small **mammals**, including scurrying mice and swooping bats, spread a plant's reproductive cells.

Words to Know

pollination: transferring male pollen to the female stigma.

self-pollination: when a plant's pollen falls onto its own stigma.

cross-pollination: when pollen from one plant transfers to the stigma of another plant.

mammal: a warm-blooded animal, such as a human, dog or cat, that can keep itself warm. Mammals feed milk to their young and usually have hair or fur covering most of their skin.

Imagine a yellow jacket as it bobs and weaves through a flower field and hovers over a burst of blooms. The insect perches on a flower's soft petals and sips nectar, a plant's sugary liquid. When it crawls inside to get nectar from the pistil, powdery pollen clings to the yellow jacket's fuzzy hind legs. As the yellow jacket buzzes off to drink another flower's nectar, pollen from the first flower settles onto the stigma of the next to fertilize the ovules.

Did you know...

Do you have any allergies? Many people are allergic to pollen. Some plants don't need pollinators. On their own, they scatter pollen into the winds. These wind-pollinated plants don't use brightly colored petals or sweet nectar to lure pollinators. Instead, they produce lots and lots of pollen to blow to nearby plants . . . and right up your nose. *Achoo*!

The Seed: Packed for the Trip of a Lifetime

The seed is a suitcase of life packed by the parent plant. Inside is everything a new plant needs to spread roots, grow strong, and develop into an adult. The **embryo** is the baby plant, in its earliest stages of development. On the outside, the **seed coat** keeps the seed from getting dried out or waterlogged.

Words to Know

embryo: a tiny plant inside a seed.

seed coat: the hard protective covering on a seed.

radicle: the first part of a plant embryo that emerges and forms a root.

plumule: the part of a plant embryo that forms a shoot.

germinate: to sprout and begin to grow.

Can you locate a seed's hilum? The seed was once attached to a plant's ovary. The hilum is a light-colored scar left on the seed after it separates. That's what you're looking for.

Inside are the **radicle** and **plumule**. As the seed **germinates**, the radicle pops out. It becomes the baby plant's first root. Other roots branch out. They develop as the plant grows and changes. The plumule provides the baby plant's first shoot. In time, the shoot becomes a stem and leaves.

PLUMULE

HILUM

RADICLE

COTYLEDON

SEED COAT

Cotyledons, the first leaves the plant produces, are like a lunch bag. Their food storage tissues contain a stash of food. The baby plant uses the stored food until it has enough leaves to begin photosynthesis to produce its own meals. When the plant develops into an adult, flowers blossom to attract pollinators. The plant's life cycle rolls on and on!

Words to Know

cotyledon: the first leaves produced by a seed.

dissect: to cut something apart to study what's inside.

anatomy: the internal structure of an organism.

Nature Detective

You can **dissect** a flower to investigate its **anatomy**. Check first to make sure a bee or other pollinator isn't inside or buzzing around! Pick a flower at peak bloom. Daffodils, gladiolus, lilies, and tulips make great specimens, but irises and roses don't work as well. With your fingers, gently pluck away the petals one by one. How are they designed to attract pollinators? Remove other parts. Can you identify the pistil and stamen and their components? Rub pollen between your fingertips. What is its texture?

Stinging Nettle

The stinging nettle is a flowering plant that gets pesky gnawing animals to leave them alone. It does this by zapping invaders, including you, with burning chemicals from dagger-like hairs on leaves and stems. But stinging nettles are not all bad. The leaves, seeds, and roots are all edible, and highly nutritious. The leaves are higher in iron than spinach, and are also high in calcium and other vitamins and minerals. Lots of people love stinging nettle soup! Does your local market sell stinging nettle tea?

Planet Protector

Many wildflowers sprout in protected areas. You might not be aware of which areas are protected. Before you uproot any wildflowers and plants, remember to find out if you are in a protected area and get permission first.

Tropism: Response to Stimulus

Try It!

Tropism means "movement." Photo means "light." Geo means "earth" and thigmo means "touch." Combine word parts to create picture definitions that illustrate different types of tropism.

Indoors, you might have observed a houseplant's leaves bent toward sunlight streaming from a window. Outdoors, you've probably seen twisty vines coiled around a garden stake, chain fence, or tree. Unlike animals, plants are fixed in place. So what's going on? Are plants moving when you're not watching?

It only seems that way!

A plant's growth is affected by **tropism**, which is an automatic response to a **stimulus**. A stimulus causes an organism to react. Stimulus and response is similar to cause and effect.

For example, when you go outside into bright sunlight, the pupils of your eyes dilate and become smaller. The stimulus, which is the light, causes the response, which is dilation. You don't control the response. It happens on its own, automatically.

Gravity, light, and water impact plant growth.

Have you wondered why a plant's roots grow downward? It's the result of **geotropism**. The force of gravity pulls roots down into the soil. **Phototropism** causes a plant to grow toward a light source.

Auxin, a plant **hormone**, causes leaves to bend and elongate, or get longer. Leaves lengthen and stretch to snatch more rays. Auxin in a climbing plant's tendril makes shoots longer and stronger. Through **thigmotropism**, a plant responds to something it touches. So a tendril coils around a branch when it feels it, or it loops around a trellis, flowerpot, or other surface.

Words to Know

tropism: a plant's involuntary response to a change in its environment.

stimulus: a change in an organism's environment that causes an action, activity, or response.

gravity: a force that pulls all objects to the earth.

geotropism: plant growth in response to the force of gravity, which makes the roots grow toward the earth.

phototropism: plant growth in response to light, which makes the leaves grow or bend toward a light source.

auxin: a chemical in a plant that causes leaves to bend and lengthen.

hormone: a chemical in a plant that controls functions like plant growth and fruit ripening.

thigmotropism: the response of a plant to physical contact.

YOU ARE MY SUNSHINE

Investigate photosynthesis! Compare the growth of a plant's leaves when they receive different amounts of sunlight. How does each respond to light stimulus?

Caution: Select a plant large enough to isolate three sections of leaves. If you can't find one, then try using three different plants of the same species. You'll observe the leaves for almost a week, so choose a field site where your project can remain undisturbed.

. . . .

1 Start a scientific method worksheet in you science journal. Draw a three-column chart and label the columns: Direct Sunlight, Indirect Sunlight, No Sunlight.

2 Select a large outdoor plant in your backyard or field site. With the ruler, measure three sections of clustered leaves that are roughly the same size. For example, if you use a garden tomato plant, then you might measure three, 5-inch leaf clusters (12½ centimeters).

3 Choose one leaf cluster to represent each column of your chart. In the appropriate column, note the length and width of the individual leaves of the clusters. Count and write down the number of healthy leaves. Draw an illustration of each section of leaves.

4 Lightly wind a twist tie around your Direct Sunlight cluster, right at the point where the leaves connect with the stem. Make sure the tie isn't too tight.

Just for Fun

Q: What did the speedy tomato say to the slowpoke tomato?

A: "C'mon, ketchup!"

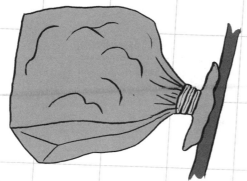

Supplies

- science journal and pencil
- large outdoor plant with leaves
- ruler
- 3 twist ties
- small brown paper bag
- colored cellophane
- sunlight

5 Place the brown bag over the No Sunlight cluster, and secure the open end of the bag with a twist tie.

6 Wrap colored cellophane around the Indirect Sunlight cluster and secure it with twist tie.

7 Predict what will happen to each section of leaves during a five-day period. Which do you think will show the most growth? The greatest health? Why?

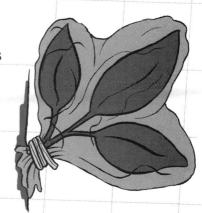

8 Observe the leaves every day, and measure them again. Take notes and make sketches in your journal. Have leaf sizes changed? Has the number of healthy leaves changed? Make an illustration of the leaves each time you check them. What conclusions do you draw about the amount of sunlight plants require to photosynthesize?

Place an indoor plant on a sunny ledge for a week to explore phototropism. Observe the ways it responds to reach more sunlight. In what ways does the plant bend and stretch for maximum exposure? How long does it take to respond? Then, search for evidence of thigmotropism outdoors. Can you find a climbing vine coiled around a surface or object? You can also plant flower seeds and snap a photo every day as the flowers grow and change until they fully bloom. Create a time-lapse film to share the process.

Planet Protector

After you investigate the garden or yard, leave it in the same condition you found it. Or in even better condition!

EGG-CENTRIC EGGHEADS

Sprout different seeds in eggshells decorated with kooky faces and compare results!

Caution: Handling raw eggs can cause illness so wash your hands thoroughly after handling.

1 Decorate the card stock with markers. Then make two stands by forming each strip of card stock into a ring. Secure the rings with glue, and hold them in place as the glue sets.

2 Ask an adult to help you remove the tops of the eggs, pour out the contents, and wash the shells in soapy water.

3 When the eggshells have dried, carefully use colored markers and glue your bits and pieces to decorate them just for fun.

4 Use the spoon to carefully fill the eggshells with potting soil. Sprinkle grass seed in one shell and herb seeds in the other. Then, add a bit more soil to each. Prop each eggshell in its stand.

Try It!

Do you live near a beach or are you heading off to visit one? Collect a few cool shells in which to sprout seeds.

Did you know...

Earth's oldest working gardens, over 10,000 years old, bloom in New Guinea. Farmers there still use the same method of plowing soil that they've used since ancient times— snuffling pigs!

5 Add a bit of water to each shell, but don't let the soil get too soaked. Place your Eggheads in a sunny location. Keep the soil moist. Seeds sprout quickly, so the Eggheads will show off green "hair" in about a week. How did the different seeds compare?

Supplies

- two, 6-inch strips of card stock (15 centimeters)
- colored permanent markers
- glue
- 2 washed eggshells with tops removed
- bits and pieces for decorating, such as googly eyes, broken jewelry, beads, fabric, or ribbon remnants
- spoon
- ½ cup potting soil (250 milliliters)
- 1 teaspoon grass seeds
- 1 teaspoon herb seeds
- water

Nature Detective

Fruits and cones are like armor that provide protection for seeds. Take apart an apple or an orange, an acorn, walnut, or pinecone. Use your fingers or small tools to discover what's packed inside.

Just for Fun

Q: What does an Egghead do when you tell it a joke?

A: It cracks up!

A-MAZING!
PHOTOTROPISM IN A SHOEBOX

Sometimes, because they're fixed in place, we forget plants are living things. They don't move. Or do they? Build a maze inside a shoebox. Observe what happens when a bean plant tries to grow toward a light source.

1 To sprout seedlings, fill the pot or cup with soil and plant the bean seeds. Lightly water the soil, and place the cup in a sunny location for one week. Keep the soil moist.

2 While you're waiting for the beans to sprout, prepare the maze. Paint the inside of the shoebox black. Allow the paint to dry completely. Draw a circle at one end of the box and cut it out.

3 Use cardboard to cut out three panels approximately half the box width in size. Stand the box vertically with the end containing the circle facing up. Place the plant temporarily inside the box, at the bottom, to make sure you allow enough room for it. Arrange the cardboard panels inside the box to form a maze. Remove the plant. Tape the panels securely in place.

4 When your beans have sprouted, stand the maze vertically, with the circle up. Place the plant in position at the bottom of the maze. Secure the cover on the box.

5 Place the box on a window ledge or in a direct source of sunlight for two weeks. Start a scientific method worksheet in your science journal. Open the lid every day to check on the plant. Keep the soil moist but not drenched.

6 What a-mazing plant responses do you observe? Is your bean plant growing? In what direction? How would you describe the way your plant is growing?

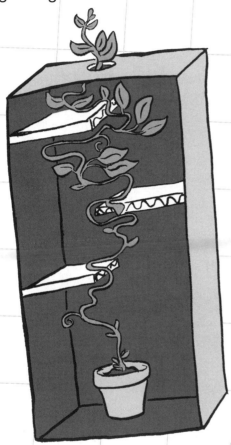

Supplies

- small pot or cup
- potting soil
- 3 bean seeds
- water
- shoebox with a lid
- black paint
- paintbrush
- pencil
- scissors
- cardboard
- duct tape
- scientific journal and pencil

Nature Detective

Hunt for evidence of phototropism in a forest preserve or wooded area. You might observe plants sprouting on the forest floor. Are they lengthened toward a better environmental condition for growth? Can you find seedlings sprouting in shade from larger plants? What twists and turns do seedlings make to lengthen toward sunlight?

Sprout a second bean plant as a control. Place the second plant next to the maze, in the same light source. Compare and contrast results after two weeks.

HEY, GEOTROPISM! WHICH WAY DO I GROW?

Sprout bean plants inside clear cups. Hypothesize what will happen as gravitational pull works its wonders!

● ●

1 Crumple the paper towel so it fits inside the cup. Pour water over the towel so it's thoroughly wet but not drenched.

2 Press the bean seeds between the towel and the side of the cup. This makes a window for you to peek through as the beans sprout! Arrange the seeds in three different positions; for example, tilted, vertical, and horizontal.

3 Start a scientific method worksheet in your science journal. Write an overall **hypothesis** about growth from different seeds. How will gravity impact root growth? In which direction or directions will roots grow?

4 Assess your hypothesis after you observe growth for two weeks. Check your seeds every day. Add water when necessary to keep the paper towel wet.

Supplies

- paper towel
- clear plastic cup
- water
- 3 pinto beans
- water
- science journal and pencil

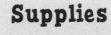

Words to Know

hypothesis: a prediction or unproven idea that tries to explain certain facts or observations.

74

Chapter 6

Adaptations Are
a Matter of Life and Death

Along with its diversity of plants, Earth enjoys an amazing abundance of animal life. Over the ages, animals have adapted for survival in unique environments. They adapt by developing physical or behavioral traits that help them to stay alive and reproduce. Physical traits are related to the body. Owls, for example, are adapted with powerful **talons** that can pierce their prey's skull.

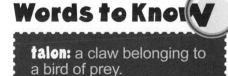

Words to Know

talon: a claw belonging to a bird of prey.

75

Behavioral traits are a certain way of acting. The hognose snake rolls over, shows its belly, and plays dead to baffle predators like hawks. The snake even hangs out its tongue for dramatic effect! Adaptation is a matter of life and death. If animals did not adapt to their environments, they would die.

Did you know...

A gator's fierce jaws, packed with about 80 razor-sharp teeth, can smash mammal, bird, and fish bones. Powerhouse jaws pulverize reptile shells.

Because environments vary greatly, adaptations do too. Do you live in the steamy Florida Everglades? You don't expect to spy an Arctic fox slinking through the swamps. The Arctic fox is a mammal and a member of the dog family. As a predator of voles and lemmings and prey to snowy owls and polar bears, the fox adapts to winter by transforming its light, brownish-gray summer coat into a lush, white coat.

Camouflaging fur is an invisibility cloak. It allows the fox to blend in with snowy surroundings.

This helps the Arctic fox to hunt rodents and dodge a predator's choppers! In bitter winds and blinding blizzards, the Arctic fox tunnels deep into the snow. It hunkers in these burrows for shelter from storms.

Do you live in Alaska's tundra? You don't expect to encounter an armor-plated alligator there. This giant reptile grows over 11 feet long (3 meters) and weighs as much as a ton.

It's adapted for survival in the Everglades' intense sunshine and heat. These carnivores are lurkers! Motionless gators spy on prey with eyes that peer out just above the surface of marshy waters. When unsuspecting prey such as a swimming turtle or a flying gull comes within range, the predator quickly attacks. It can even grab a raccoon scuttling up a swooping tree limb. The gator lunges 5 feet into the air (1½ meters) to snatch its prey and swallow it whole.

Nature Detective

Quietly observe animals adapted to survive with camouflage. Look for berries, vines, and leaves. Perhaps you'll encounter a walking stick blending with twigs as it chomps lunch. Do you spot a rock rustling? Maybe it's a toad camouflaged in the dirt.

Predator-Prey Relationships

Predator-prey relationships keep Earth's ecosystems thriving. They maintain balance among incredibly diverse species. Predators constantly prowl for meat. They are adapted to hunt and kill for survival. Prey are adapted with **defense mechanisms** to leap out of a predator's jaws.

Words to Know

defense mechanism: a way to protect oneself.

Consider the endangered Florida panther and the white-tailed deer. Predator and prey. The panther is adapted to hunt animals and devour meat. The magnificent big cat reigns at the top of the Everglades food chain. A secretive, solitary carnivore, the panther slinks through swamplands. How does the stealthy predator sneak up on its favorite prey? Tufts of fur and webbed skin between its toes muffle sound. Add motion-detecting whiskers, a keen sense of smell, stellar night vision, and swiveling ears that zone in on a deer rustling through the brush.

Did you know...

Panthers don't live in **congregations**. They're loners and only join others to **mate**. Even mothers only live with kittens temporarily, until the young panthers can survive on their own.

When the panther pounces, powerful shoulder and neck muscles and weighty jawbones take the shock from the tackle. Taking down large prey is hazardous. A deer's sharp hooves could **gore** the panther. The carnivore relies on a quick kill. Sharp fangs pierce the deer's neck and strong teeth rip at the meat. A tongue covered with horny tips cuts like scissors. After feeding, the panther drags the carcass under a tree. It heaps leaves and dirt over the leftovers to conceal them from **scavengers**. The panther will return for future meals.

Sometimes, the predator isn't successful.

The fleet-footed white-tailed deer is adapted with speed and leaping skill to elude the panther's attack. As the panther lunges, the agile deer can bound on long legs over an 8-foot tree trunk (2½ meters) and tear through swamplands at 40 miles per hour (64 kilometers per hour).

Words to Know

congregation: a group of animals.

mate: to reproduce.

gore: to pierce an animal's flesh.

scavenger: an animal, bird, or insect that eats rotting food or animals that are already dead.

habitat: the natural area where a plant or animal lives.

endangered: a plant or animal species with a dangerously low population.

The deer is also a skilled swimmer, and it can jump into deep water to throw the predator off its scent. Confused, the panther gives up. It whiffs the scent of an armadillo and slinks away to trail a not-so-favorite meal.

Did you know...

Sadly, after years of **habitat** loss, being hunted, and vehicle accidents, the Florida panther population has shrunk. The National Wildlife Federation reports only about 80 **endangered** panthers remain in the wild.

Critter Congregations

Have you heard of a herd? That's a congregation of bison. You might have spotted a gaggle of geese or an army of frogs in your nature investigations. Different animals have different names for their groups. Which critter congregations are native to your area?

Animal	Class	Congregation	Animal	Class	Congregation
badgers	mammal	cete, clan	hawks	bird	cast
bats	mammal	colony	herons	bird	sedge
bears	mammal	sloth	otters	mammal	romp
bobolinks	bird	chain	owls	bird	parliament
buzzards	bird	wake	porcupines	mammal	prickle
cranes	bird	sedge	rabbits	mammal	warren, colony
crocodiles	reptile	bask	seals	mammal	pod, herd
crows	bird	murder, horde	sharks	fish	shiver
ducks	bird	flock	snakes	reptile	nest
eagles	bird	convocation	squirrels	mammal	dray, scurry
elk	mammal	gang	swans	bird	bevy
flamingos	bird	stand	toads	amphibian	knot
foxes	mammal	leash, skulk	turkeys	bird	rafter
goats	mammal	tribe	whales	mammal	pod
gulls	bird	colony	wolves	mammal	pack

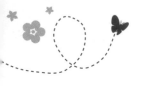

The Performing Stoat

The stoat is a sleek-bodied member of the weasel family. It lives in Europe, New Zealand, and North America. A slim package of energy, the predator takes down prey 10 times its size with a bizarre hunting strategy! Outside rabbit **warrens**, the carnivore dances a crazy jig. The stoat twists, twirls, and boings into the air. Curious rabbits pop out of hiding to gawk at the acrobatic show. Suddenly, the stoat pounces, killing a mesmerized rabbit with one swift bite to the throat.

Gross-Out Animal Defenses

In nature's wild world, it's all about survival. How do prey keep from becoming dinner? Some defenses are out-and-out gross. Prey fling goop, slime, and blood at predators. *Ew!*

The fulmar is a seabird native to Newfoundland, the British Isles, and the Arctic Circle. It resembles a gull. In fact, fulmar means "foul gull." No wonder. It's adapted with a disgusting defense: vomit! When threatened, the fulmar **projectile**-barfs on enemies with an oily, fishy glop of stinky vomit. Bright orange goop smacks predators as far as 5 feet away (1½ meters). The reeking stuff isn't only gross. It's also dangerous. **Acidic** vomit gnaws away at the waterproof coating on an enemy's feathers.

Words to Know

warren: burrows where rabbits live.

projectile: to hurl, launch, or blast forward.

acidic: bitter, tart, or sour.

The hagfish is a nearly blind, eel-like fish. A scavenger that feasts on rotting flesh from dead fish, it lives in oceans around the globe.

A jawless mouth, circled by tentacles, holds two sets of thorny teeth. Swimming underwater, the hagfish looks like easy pickings for ravenous sharks. But it's packing a creepy defense. Slime!

What happens when a shark clamps its huge jaws on the hagfish?

Thick slime oozes from hundreds of pores on the fish's body. It swirls into a gooey "cocoon" that surrounds the hagfish. In seconds, gunky slime clogs the fierce predator's gills. Gagging, the suffocating shark retreats. So, how does the hagfish escape its own slimy clutches? With an amazing rope trick! It ties itself into a knot. The fish shivers the knot down its thin body all the way to its tail as it wrings the gunk away.

The Texas horned lizard is less than 3 inches long (7 centimeters), but it has enormous defenses. The lizard resembles a mini dragon with a scaly body spiked with prickly thorns. This armor is great camouflage in deserts, and makes the lizard tricky for hungry bobcats, coyotes, or snakes to eat. But that's not all. This tiny reptile squirts blood out of miniature blood vessels in its bulging eyes. As if blood isn't nasty enough, it's flavored with poisonous chemicals, probably because of the horned lizard's favorite snack—**venomous** ants! Blinded and baffled by the vile squirting blood, most predators scram.

Words to Know

venomous: poisonous.

Seasonal Adaptations

As winter approaches, chipmunks behave by hoarding secret stashes. They **stockpile** nuts and acorns to survive lean times. Other animals handle the winter by **hibernating**. Imagine a bear all cozy and warm in its den, sleeping through the long, cold winter.

Some animals have to escape bitter temperatures and icy snows by **migrating**. Migration is a behavioral adaptation. Monarch butterflies set off on marathon flights from the eastern and midwestern parts of the United States and flutter all the way to balmy climates in Guatemala, Honduras, and Mexico.

Nature Detective

Every environment enjoys its own unique characteristics. Do you live in a tropical place like Honolulu, Hawaii? The temperature probably doesn't change much. As the American city with the least seasonal change, Honolulu's average temperature is 77 degrees Fahrenheit (25 degrees Celsius). Perhaps you live in an area that experiences dramatic seasonal changes and a wide range of temperatures. How do you adapt as winter sweeps in? Maybe you bundle up in layers and yank on mittens and toasty boots to explore snowy environments. How do animals adapt to seasonal changes where you live? As you observe animals in the wild, notice physical and behavioral traits that help them survive.

Words to Know

stockpile: to store large amounts of something for later use. Also called hoarding.

hibernate: to sleep through the winter in a cave or underground.

migrate: to move from one environment to another when seasons change.

overwinter: to survive the winter by remaining in an environment.

antifreeze: a liquid that is added to a second liquid to lower the temperature at which the second liquid freezes.

Did you know...

California boasts the United States' strictest laws about animals that cannot be kept as pets. Ferrets, hedgehogs, and sugar gliders, common pets in many regions, are banned there. The California Department of Fish and Game says, "Ferrets … may bite in a frenzied fashion that's dangerous to small children and infants." When they escape from homes, ferrets devour wildlife, such as ground-nesting birds. Hedgehog quills can poke into skin and spread germs. When sugar gliders bust out of homes, they destroy crops. Which pets are prohibited where you live? Research your state's Division of Wildlife to find out!

Other insects, including beetles and midges, hang around. They **overwinter** with physical adaptations. Water moves out of their body's cells into spaces between the cells. In the article "Snug as a Bug in the Snow," author Michael J. Caduto discusses "biological **antifreeze**." He writes, "When water surrounding cells freezes, it is not as likely to burst cell membranes and damage tissues. At the same time, concentrated sugars and alcohols form within the cells, which lower their freezing point and keep cellular fluids from icing up."

So by moving the liquid outside the cells, these insects create a layer of protection around their cells while the insides are huddling together to keep warm.

Planet Protector

Sure, cuddly bunnies and baby raccoons, called kits, are adorable. What's not to love about fuzzy ducklings? Sweet fawns hiding from predators in meadow grasses? Sometimes it's tempting to take baby animals home as pets. We forget that in time, the 6-pound fawn (3 kilograms) becomes a 125-pound doe (57 kilograms). Raccoons can carry **rabies**, a virus harmful to people.

Just remember, wild animals are adapted for life in their own natural environments. They shouldn't be confined in cages, homes, and yards. In many areas it's against the law to remove animals from habitats and raise them in captivity. The Maryland Department of National Resources warns that "Unnatural conditions of life in captivity can lead to **malnutrition**, injury and **stress** . . . Wild animals that become accustomed to humans can pose a threat to themselves and to people." The Humane Society weighs in, too, stating in an article that, "Wild animals, by nature, are self-sufficient . . . The instinctive behavior of these animals makes them unsuitable as pets."

Words to Know

rabies: a virus of the nervous system transmitted through the bite of an infected mammal.

malnutrition: poor nutrition caused by not eating the right foods.

stress: pressure or strain, often due to changes in conditions or environments.

nonnative: a plant or animal growing or living in an environment it didn't originally come from.

invasive species: a nonnative plant or animal that harms an ecosystem.

parasite: a plant or animal that gets its nourishment from a host plant or animal, while also damaging the host.

When animals destroy furniture, relieve themselves on floors, bite, and scratch, people get frustrated. Sometimes, they return these critters to the wild, but often to completely new habitats. Release to a **nonnative** habitat might disrupt other wildlife in an ecosystem. There's greater competition for resources. **Invasive species** can devour native animals and plants and destroy crops. They impact an ecosystem's circle of life. New diseases and **parasites** can spread and new predators can overwhelm the balance of food webs.

Please leave critters in their own homes. Don't take them to yours. Keep wild animals wild!

HABITAT OBSERVATION

Grab your Nature Detective kit to observe ecosystem interactions!

1 Scout around for a habitat to observe. You might select the edge of a pond, a wooded area, a park, or a decaying log. Quietly, and without disturbing it, watch the ecosystem from both far-away and up-close perspectives. Start a scientific method worksheet in your science journal. Use the chart to record observations.

2 What types of animals and plants live in the habitat? What evidence of adaptations, such as hoarding, camouflage, and defense mechanisms do you observe? How do living and non-living things interact?

3 Sketch the plants and animals you see in the ecosystem, and use print and electronic resources to identify them.

Supplies

- Nature Detective toolkit
- science journal and pencil
- rubber gloves and garbage bags

4 Revisit the ecosystem after a change of seasons or weather conditions. For example, observe it after a rainfall or snowfall. Explore it after significant changes, such as a controlled burn, tree planting, reseeding, or flooding. What similarities and differences do you notice?

Plant Protector

How about taking along gloves and bags to clear away junk? Note ways in which trash, including plastic bags, ditched food, or bottles and cans, impact the habitat.

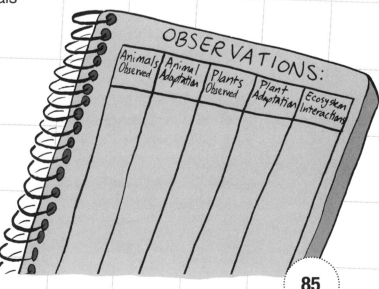

OBSERVATIONS:

Animals Observed	Animal Adaptation	Plants Observed	Plant Adaptation	Ecosystem Interactions

ANIMAL TRACKER PLASTER CASTER

What wild animals share your environment? Sometimes you're aware of them. Coyotes howl at night. Prairie dogs yip and pop from burrows. Pelicans dive-bomb churning waters. A skunk's scent burns your nostrils. Other times, animals prowl soundlessly. Track 'em down!

Caution: Ask an adult to help you cut the bottle into rings and scout for tracks. **Wear a life vest near water.**

1 Choose a squishy area to explore, preferably a place where animals drink water. You might choose a pond, creek, or stream, or even a large mud puddle. Riverbanks and sandbars work well, too.

2 It's tricky to locate a clear track in the wild. Animals are on the move and tracks get smudged. Scout for a deep track that contains a strong imprint all the way around. Study the track. Is it webbed? Does it include claws? Tail or wing imprints? Perhaps the animal left behind a bit of fur, a quill, or a feather. Lightly brush away any debris such as twigs, stones, and leaves. Don't use too much force or it will smear the track.

3 Cut the bottle into 2-inch ringed sections (5 centimeters). Center one plastic bottle ring over the track. Carefully press the ring about ½ inch into the ground (1¼ centimeters). Now you have a form to hold the plaster in place.

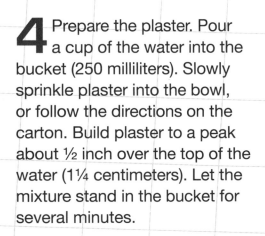

4 Prepare the plaster. Pour a cup of the water into the bucket (250 milliliters). Slowly sprinkle plaster into the bowl, or follow the directions on the carton. Build plaster to a peak about ½ inch over the top of the water (1¼ centimeters). Let the mixture stand in the bucket for several minutes.

Supplies

- 2-liter bottle
- scissors
- plaster of Paris
- small bucket or beach pail
- measuring cups
- 16-ounce plastic bottle filled with water (500 milliliters)
- old tablespoon
- shovel or garden trowel
- newspaper or bubble wrap

5 After the plaster has absorbed some of the water, slowly stir the mixture with the spoon. This is the trickiest step! Keep stirring until there are no lumps and the plaster reaches a smooth, creamy consistency. It's important to blend the mixture very slowly to avoid creating air bubbles. Air bubbles result in a less detailed cast.

6 To release any bubbles that do form, carefully rap the bottom of the bucket against a tree stump, rock, or other hard surface. Any air bubbles will rise to the top. Continue rapping until bubbles stop rising.

7 Make the cast. Pour some plaster into the ring. Make sure you don't pour plaster directly onto the track, or you may not get a good casting. Instead, pour at the side of the track and allow the plaster to ooze over the track on its own. Fill the circle to the top.

White-tailed Deer

Raccoon

Opossum

Mallard

continues on next page . . .

87

8 Allow the cast to harden completely. Depending on weather conditions, it may take 30 to 60 minutes. In the meantime, scout for other tracks. Can you identify the critters that left them?

9 When the plaster is hard, remove the cast. First, use the shovel to push aside the ground about 5 inches outside the cast (12½ centimeters). Then, dig away earth beneath the cast. Gently lift out the cast. If it doesn't lift, carefully place it back in position. Remove more earth. It might be tempting to try to jack up the cast with the shovel or a stick. But it's very fragile. Try to lift it gently with your hands so the cast doesn't crack or crumble. Use the scissors to cut away the plastic ring.

10 Wrap the fragile cast in newspaper or bubble wrap to cushion it until you get home. Then, allow it to thoroughly dry for two days. As it dries out, the cast will feel warm when you touch it. When it feels cool, clean the cast.

mallard

Use a field guide such as *Animal Tracks* by Olaus J. Murie and Mark Elbroch to identify prints.

Planet Protector

Don't leave litter behind after casting, and please remember to clean up after yourself.

FANTANIMAL

How are animals adapted for life where you live? With wedge-shaped digging structures like New Mexico's spadefoot toad? Wedges are built-in shovels to tunnel underground during pounding rains in monsoon seasons. Perhaps, like beavers that thrive across North America, animals near you have clear eyelids to see as they paddle underwater. Waterproof fur keeps them warm and dry. Take dashes of adaptations from animals in your area. Add sprinkles of imagination to create a fantasy animal built for survival!

Supplies

- paper and pencil
- Elmer's glue or other craft glue
- art paper
- beads
- buttons
- cotton balls
- fabric swatches
- feathers
- glitter
- magazines
- modeling clay
- newspaper
- paper plates
- scissors
- sequins
- shells

1 What physical and behavioral adaptations do animals need to survive in your environment? Are they adapted with camouflage to fool predators? With special ears or eyes for hunting? Zero in on adaptations you find fascinating.

2 Let your imagination run wild! Imagine what your area would be like with completely different conditions, such as year-round ice, midnight sun, or fluorescent trees.

3 Use paper and pencil to sketch a plan for a Fantanimal that features real and imagined adaptations for survival in your environment's new conditions.

4 Select items from the Supplies list, and add other odds and ends you have available. Create a model of your Fantanimal.

herbivore

camouflage

long neck

armor

webbed feet

hooves

ROLY-POLY HABITAT IN A BOX

Woodlice are tiny armored decomposers that look like insects. They have many nicknames that make them sound like bugs too—roly-poly bugs, doodlebugs, armadillo bugs, potato or pill bugs—but woodlice are actually crustaceans with seven pairs of legs. They are adapted with physical and behavioral defenses that include a hard outer skeleton with plates that cover their bodies like armor. When threatened or touched, woodlice curl into tight, protective balls.

Where can you unearth woodlice? They love soil and moisture. Scout under leaf litter, decaying plant matter, and grass clippings. They hang out in the dark under stacks of wood, piles of mulch, and clay pots, too. You can build a temporary home for a roly-poly and observe its behaviors before you release it back into its natural environment.

1 Wear gloves to prepare the habitat. Fill the box about halfway with moist soil. Save some moist soil for the next step. Spread a layer of mulch over the soil. Sprinkle a layer of oats over the mulch. Cover the top with large leaves.

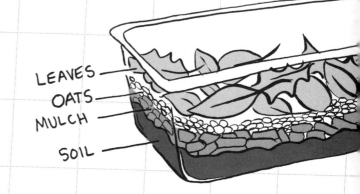

LEAVES
OATS
MULCH
SOIL

2 Prepare the transporter. Repeat the habitat preparation on a smaller scale. In the deli tub, layer moist soil and small leaves. You'll use this container to transport roly-polys.

3 Trek outdoors to scout for roly-polys. Wear gloves and use the shovel to turn over leaves and piles of twigs. Carefully flip rocks and lift logs. Gently place your roly-polys in the transporter. Note the location where you found the roly-polys, so you can return them to the same place in several days.

Did you know...

Woodlice eat scat. That's poop and animal droppings. Woodlice recycle scat straight back into the soil.

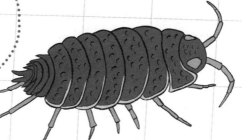

4 Gently transfer roly-polys into the habitat. Allow them to burrow into the layers, and close the lid. Observe the roly-polys for several days. Keep the soil moist, and sprinkle more oats and mulch into the habitat. Start a scientific method worksheet in your science journal. What do you think the roly-polys will spend their time doing? Will they move around a lot? Will they group together or stay separate? Record your observations and create illustrations to describe the roly-polys' activities and behaviors.

5 After the observation period, return all the roly-polys to their natural environment. Wear gloves as you gently remove layers in the habitat to unearth the critters. Place them into a fresh transporter. Then, carefully release them where you found them.

Supplies

- garden gloves
- plastic box with lid
- moist soil
- mulch such as chopped up leaves, straw or grass clippings
- oats
- several large leaves
- deli tub with lid
- several small leaves
- shovel or garden trowel
- 4–6 roly-polys
- hand lens
- science journal and pencil

Did you know...

Female woodlice carry babies in pouches like kangaroos!

Bye, Roly-poly!!

Planet Protector

Don't forget to handle roly-polys and their outside homes gently. Return the environment to its original condition by filling holes and smoothing leaf litter. Roly-polys aren't the only living things that make homes there. If you flipped over a log, you might have disturbed worms, centipedes, and more.

Chapter 7

Animal Life Cycles

The life cycle is a circle of life. Animals are born. They go through stages of development as they grow into adults. From **larva** to yellow jacket. From tadpole to frog. From egg to emu. From kit to badger. As adults, animals reproduce and replace themselves with new generations. In time, they die.

Animal Reproduction

Animals are born with a mating **instinct**. An instinct is not something an animal learns. It's a natural behavior or characteristic. Mating allows animals to produce **offspring** of their own kind. Animals die, but their offspring have replaced them. This is how a species survives and the circle of life keeps rolling.

Through **sexual reproduction**, adult animals pass **genes** onto their offspring. Babies inherit certain characteristics from each of their parents, which pass on from one generation to the next. How does sexual reproduction take place? Female and male animals produce sex cells. Females produce egg cells. Males produce sperm cells.

Words to Know

larva: the worm-like stage of an insect's life. Plural is larvae.

instinct: an inborn behavior, need, or characteristic.

offspring: an animal's young.

sexual reproduction: reproduction that joins male and female cells.

genes: basic units in our cells that carry characteristics from one generation to the next.

fertilization: the joining of male sperm cells and female egg cells.

Through **fertilization**, which is the union of male and female reproductive cells, the egg begins to develop. It changes and grows into a baby.

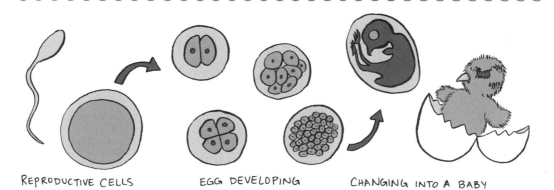

REPRODUCTIVE CELLS   EGG DEVELOPING   CHANGING INTO A BABY

Attracting a Mate

Before reproducing, animals compete to attract mates. They engage in mating rituals. To dazzle females, male peacocks strut and show off shimmery tail plumage. Male fiddler crabs waggle enlarged claws to attract females—and to warn rivals to scram! Adapted for nightlife with **bioluminescence**, fireflies flash lights in a special pattern.

Words to Know

bioluminescence: a chemical reaction that allows fireflies to produce their own light.

cannibal: an animal that eats its own species.

Competition is often ferocious. Some animals, including the moose, battle for a partner. One-ton males, called bulls, clash for females, called cows. Two grunting, snorting bulls smash and slam their huge, branched antlers together. The bashing continues until one battered fighter hustles away. Then the victor claims his mate.

Female warriors tussle too. Chir-lee, chir-lee! That's the call of an Eastern bluebird. Scrappy females are extremely aggressive. They not only fight over mates, but also over prime nesting sites. Using its short beak as a weapon, one female pecks another to death.

Did you know...

Some females are **cannibals**! Female black widow spiders, jumping spiders, and praying mantises sometimes kill and gobble partners after mating.

Natural Selection

Not all males and females reproduce. Only certain males and females win the opportunity to mate. Male Mormon crickets are fussy. They turn away females with lighter weights and choose heavier ones. It makes good sense for them! Heavier females bear more offspring, which means they produce more Mormon crickets.

Why is competition so fierce? It's essential for reproduction. When animals fail to win mates, they don't reproduce. What happens when animals don't reproduce? They don't pass genetic traits to a new generation. They are unable to impact the future generations of their species. If the heavier crickets are passing on their genes, their offspring are likely to be heavy too.

Charles Darwin (1809–1882) was a naturalist who wrote *The Origin of Species*. According to Darwin's theory of **natural selection**, animals best adapted for survival in their environments win chances to reproduce. They pass along their beneficial traits to the next generation. Some of those offspring survive, reproduce, and carry on the cycle.

Did you know...

Made of the chemical DNA (DeoxyriboNucleic Acid), **chromosomes** contain the genes that give living things their characteristics. DNA, in the form of a double pair of twisted strands that look like a crooked ladder, is an important messenger. It carries genetic information from one generation to the next.

Words to Know

chromosome: a rod-shaped structure in a cell nucleus that carries genes.

natural selection: the process that allows organisms best adapted for an environment to reproduce.

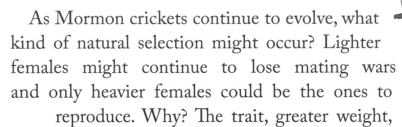

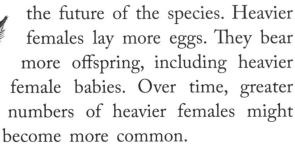

As Mormon crickets continue to evolve, what kind of natural selection might occur? Lighter females might continue to lose mating wars and only heavier females could be the ones to reproduce. Why? The trait, greater weight, has a genetic basis. It's an advantage for the future of the species. Heavier females lay more eggs. They bear more offspring, including heavier female babies. Over time, greater numbers of heavier females might become more common.

Nature Detective

Some animals, including birds, **reptiles**, **amphibians**, insects, and fish are **oviparous**. They lay eggs that hatch into offspring outside the mother's body. Other animals, like most mammals, are **viviparous**. They bear live offspring. Explore your environment for evidence of oviparous and viviparous critters.

Words to Know

reptile: a cold-blooded animal, like a snake or lizard, that needs sunlight to keep warm and shade to stay cool. It crawls on its belly or on short legs.

amphibian: a cold-blooded animal, such as a toad, frog or salamander, that needs sunlight to keep warm and shade to stay cool. Amphibians live on land and in the water.

oviparous: an animal that lays eggs.

viviparous: an animal that has live births.

Did you know....

There are 'parous exceptions! The duck-billed platypus and spiny anteater of Australia and New Guinea are egg-laying mammals. Guppies and sharks don't lay eggs like other fish—they bear live offspring.

FINE-FEATHERED FRIENDS

activity

Birds build nests where they lay and hatch eggs, and where their offspring can grow. Collect twigs, moss, dandelion fluff, and other natural elements to build a nest that will actually attract birds!

1 Nature-detect to discover the nests that birds build in your field site. Please avoid disturbing nesting birds. When exploring, wear garden gloves and gather materials to build your nest. Store mud in plastic containers, and place materials in the collection bag.

2 Consider the type of nest to build. Create a scientific method worksheet in your science journal to help you plan your nest. What species will hatch in your nest? Which building materials does the species prefer? How heavy and secure will the nest need to be? Pose other questions to help your planning.

3 Locate a low-slung, forked tree branch. Using only your hands and the natural elements, build a nest in the fork. Use mud to pack building materials together. It's not easy. But many birds do the job with only their beaks!

4 Test the nest. Place pebbles inside to represent eggs. Is the nest strong enough to support them? What adjustments can you make to build a sturdier nest?

Supplies

- garden gloves
- dandelion fluff
- dried grass
- dog or other fur
- feathers
- moss
- mud
- pine needles
- twigs
- small shovel or trowel
- plastic containers
- collection bag
- science journal and pencil
- pebbles

METAMORPHO-PLATE

Complete **metamorphosis** is a series of changes that many organisms go through as they develop. Through physical changes, the newborn and the adult look nothing alike. Babies that go through a complete metamorphosis are total transformers! Create a life cycle model that illustrates transformation from egg to monarch butterfly.

Hint: If you'd like, paint each type of pasta a different color!

Words to Know

metamorphosis: an animal's complete change in physical form as it develops into an adult.

1 Make a circle of change. Use scissors to cut the sheet of colored paper into a circle that fits the inner section of the paper plate. Fold the circle in half, and firmly press the edge between your fingers. Fold it in half again, and press the second edge.

2 Unfold and flatten the circle. You should see four pie-slice sections. Use the marker to trace over the fold lines. Glue the paper in the center of the paper plate. Hold the paper flat until it sticks.

Try It!

Watch the fantastic film "Complete Life Cycle of the Monarch Butterfly," from the Chicago Nature Museum in Chicago, Illinois! www.youtube.com/watch?v=7AUeM8Mbalk

3 On the plate's rim, label the four sections: Egg, Caterpillar, Chrysalis, Butterfly.

4 Time for the egg! Glue one piece of orzo onto a leaf. As the orzo dries, glue a twig in the Egg section. Then glue the leaf with the orzo so it hangs from the twig.

5 The next stage is the caterpillar. Glue one piece of rotini in the center of another leaf. Make a twig perch for it, and glue it in place in the Caterpillar section.

6 The caterpillar has morphed into a chrysalis! Glue the last twig into the Chrysalis section. Glue the conghiglie so it hangs from the twig.

7 When the metamorphosis is complete, the butterfly emerges! Glue the flower into the Butterfly section. Place the farfalle in flight over it.

Supplies

- scissors
- sheet of colored paper
- large paper plate
- permanent marker
- Elmer's glue or other craft glue
- dried pasta: orzo (seed-shaped), rotini (corkscrew-shaped), conghiglie (shell-shaped), farfalle (bowtie-shaped)
- 2 leaves
- 3 twigs
- 1 flower

Did you know...

Farfalla is the Italian word for butterfly! Other words for butterfly include mariposa in Spanish, papillon in French, schmetterling in German, and borboleta in Portuguese.

Chapter 8

Protect Living Things

Around and around it goes! Earth's enormous circle of life links all living things. In nature's interconnected cycles, many of our actions launch a chain of events that can sometimes harm living things. In your own outdoor investigations, you've probably noticed people's impact on the environment.

100

Have you seen plastic bags billowing like ghosts from jam-packed trash cans? Maybe you've spotted gnarled fishing line, crushed bait containers, and squashed plastic bottles bobbing in a lake. Or have you seen a single lonely boot ditched under a picnic table? What you might not realize is how all of our actions impact an ecosystem's food chain, and reach ecosystems far away.

Pollutants Flow Through the Food Chain

Bioaccumulation is the buildup of harmful substances inside the tissue of living things. Because living things are connected through food chains, this buildup passes along. And it increases as it goes. Through **biomagnification**, harmful substances become more concentrated as they move up a food chain.

Imagine an ocean ecosystem. First, hazardous chemicals leak into the environment from a nearby processing plant. Then they ooze over land, contaminating beaches. They seep into the water, spreading pollution.

Words to Know

bioaccumulation: the buildup of harmful substances inside the tissues of living things.

biomagnification: the process through which harmful substances become more concentrated as they pass up a food chain.

Plankton, the first link in marine food chains, soak up these chemicals. Shrimp nibble the plankton—and take in the chemicals stored in the plankton's tissues. Next, a cuttlefish devours the shrimp. A shark scarfs the cuttlefish. Toxic buildups increase. Chemicals move through the chain, growing more intense at each level.

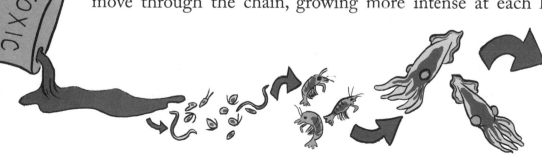

101

Our actions can impact living things thousands of miles from where we live. Photographers David Liittschwager and Susan Middleton wrote *Archipelago: Portraits of Life in the World's Most Remote Island Sanctuary*. In researching their book, they visited **remote** coral reefs in the Hawaiian Islands. Every day as they entered their studio, they greeted a young albatross. They nicknamed him Shed Bird. Soon, the seabird would be heading out of its mother's nest. The young albatross would strike out alone, soar over the sea, and take care of itself.

Tragically, Shed Bird never had the chance to spread his wings.

Words to Know

remote: far-away and isolated.

ingest: to swallow.

debris: litter.

His parents, swooping over waves to snag squid, ended up also **ingesting** rubbish. From the sky, bits of balloons, chunks of broken toys, glittering disposable lighters, and bobbing bottle caps looked like food. When his parents regurgitated the food to feed their baby, Shed Bird swallowed the **debris**. The young albatross died from our garbage.

Did you know...

Researchers from NOAA (National Oceanic and Atmospheric Administration) who studied seals off the coast of Alaska's Pribilof Islands observed more than 800 seals snarled in fishing line, plastic beverage bands, and other trash. In some cases, scientists were able to free the marine mammals. In other cases, though, removing dug-in plastic junk could harm some seals. Scientists were forced to let many seals go without providing help.

Where does all this trash come from? Maybe it fluttered out of a recycling truck. Winds blew it miles away. Or someone accidentally kicked a crushed plastic spoon into a storm grate. You might think that one piece of litter today doesn't matter. But all the bits of trash add up to so much trash that it's clogging our oceans.

Keep It Rolling!

Nature shares its gifts with us. It provides everything we need to survive, grow, change, and flourish. You've been exploring nature. Perhaps it's been in your own backyard. What wondrous plants and animals did you encounter? Earth's abundant gifts are all around us. Sometimes we think they're limitless. We assume they'll be around for the generations that will replace us. It's easy to take for granted the air we breathe, food we eat, and water we drink. Even the fuel we consume.

How about giving something back?

Perhaps you can select an area of a park or playground and clear away garbage regularly. Pitch in to clean up a creek or pond. Clear invasive plants from a nature center. Rally friends to plant trees. Organize a litter-free lunch. Imagine the impact you'll make. It's for your future, for your planet's future, and for the circle of life.

ORGANIZE A CLEANUP!

Just one person makes a difference in protecting living things. Imagine the impact a group can make! Select an outdoor area, such as a nature trail, forest preserve, or creek. Develop a plan to work with others to spruce it up.

Hint: Don't forget to get permission from city officials, park services, or private owners before you start.

● ●

1 Plan! Rally friends, family, and your community. Encourage people to protect, defend, and restore nature with a cleanup. Set a date and time for the event.

2 Publicize! Design clever, colorful flyers and posters you can hang to spread the word. If you're part of a school blog, post "before" photos from the cleanup site. Host a podcast to rally others. Contact a local news group to share an article about the cleanup.

3 Gather supplies! Ask for donations of cleaning supplies, such as leaf and yard waste recycling bags and garbage bags. Collect tongs for picking up sharp items and rubber and gardening gloves to protect hands.

4 Clean up! Greet volunteers and thank them for joining you. Ask volunteers to be aware of broken bottles and other sharp materials they shouldn't touch. As everyone cleans, set aside recyclables, including bottles, cans, and newspapers, to take to a recycling center. Collect trash in bags for disposal. Don't forget to clear away any trash that volunteers generate, such as empty water bottles or snack wrappers.

5 Debrief! Afterward, evaluate the event. How many volunteers pitched in? What changes can improve the next cleanup? If you performed a podcast or wrote a blog, update it with "after" photos. Add action shots of enthusiastic volunteers.

Congratulations on a job well done!

Traveling Trash

The devastating earthquake and tsunami that hit Japan in March 2011 killed more than 15,000 people and left over 130,000 homeless. And it swept about 5 million tons of debris into the Pacific Ocean. The debris from the tsunami could have a major impact on wildlife in the Pacific Ocean. The televisions, washing machines, refrigerators, and other appliances floating in the water carry harmful chemicals. If the trash reaches the shores of Hawaii, it could damage reefs, introduce invasive species, and impact the Laysan and black-footed albatross, Hawaiian monk seal, green sea turtle, and other threatened and endangered species. Floating fishing gear could threaten seabirds and migratory Pacific species like bluefin tuna, green and leatherback sea turtles, mako and blue sharks, and whales that use North Pacific waters to feed, breed, and migrate. Some scientists predict that tons of trash will hit the coasts of California, Washington, British Columbia, and Alaska in 2013.

EDIBLE CORAL REEF

Teeming with life, coral reefs are aquatic ecosystems. They are homes to thousands of species. According to NOAA, scientists estimate there may be up to 8 million undiscovered species thriving in coral reefs. Water pollution, overfishing, and climate change threaten reefs' weird and wonderful creatures. Bake a cake to share what you know about ocean life!

Be Careful: Ask an adult to help you with the oven and raw eggs.

1 Don't forget to wash your hands before you begin. Prepare the sheet cake. Preheat the oven to 350 degrees Fahrenheit (175 degrees Celsius). In one bowl, combine the sugar and butter until they reach a creamy consistency. Add the first egg. Thoroughly blend. Repeat with the second egg. Blend in vanilla extract. In a second bowl, combine flour, baking soda, and salt. Add it bit by bit to the first mixture. As you stir the dry ingredients into the mixture, add milk. Combine until the batter is smooth.

2 Carefully pour the mixture into the greased pan. Use a spatula to scrape batter from the bowl. Bake for about 40 minutes. Ovens are quirky! After 30 minutes, check your cake's progress. It will be ready when it bounces back after you press it lightly with your fingertips. Wear mitts when you remove the pan from the oven.

3 While the cake cools, prepare the icing. In a fresh mixing bowl, cream butter until it's fluffy. Gradually stir in powdered sugar, milk, and vanilla. Mix thoroughly. Slowly add drops of blue food coloring to create the ocean's water. If the icing is too thin or too thick, add more powdered sugar or more milk in small quantities.

4 When the cake is cool, frost and decorate it. Completely cover the surface with blue icing. At one end of the cake, sprinkle crushed graham crackers to represent a sand bar. Combine coconut and green food coloring to make sea grass. Add it to the ocean waters. Arrange licorice whips for branches of coral, and add sponge cake for, well, sponges!

5 How about more sea creatures? Add gummy fish. Dried cranberries represent sea urchins. Use your imagination to think of other items to represent ocean inhabitants—even undiscovered ones!

6 Share the cake with family and friends. As you dig in, also share what you know about the ways our actions impact nature.

Supplies

- oven
- mixing bowls
- wooden spoons
- measuring spoons
- measuring cups
- greased 9-by-9-inch baking pan (23 by 23 centimeters)
- spatulas
- oven mitts

Cake Ingredients

- 1 cup sugar (225 grams)
- ½ cup softened unsalted butter (115 grams)
- 2 eggs
- 2 tablespoons vanilla extract (30 milliliters)
- 1½ cups flour (165 grams)
- 1 tablespoon baking soda (15 milliliters)
- ¾ teaspoon salt (15 milliliters)
- ½ cup milk (125 milliliters)

Icing Ingredients

- ⅓ cup softened unsalted butter (75 grams)
- 3 cups powdered sugar (330 grams)
- 2 tablespoons milk (30 milliliters)
- 2 teaspoons vanilla extract (30 milliliters)
- blue food coloring

Ingredients for Decorations

- crushed graham crackers
- shredded coconut
- green food coloring
- licorice whips
- sponge cake, cut into bite-sized pieces
- gummy fish
- dried cranberries

EXPERIMENT WITH WETLAND PLANT POLLUTION

Make predictions and compare results! Water one outdoor fern plant, a typical plant found in wetlands, with polluted water. Water a second with its runoff. How will pollutants impact growth?

1 Start a scientific method worksheet in your science journal, then prepare the plants. With the marker, write Wetland 1 and Wetland 2 on the labels. Attach one label to each fern. Measure each plant's height. Record the measurements on your worksheet. Write a description of each plant's health.

2 Place a saucer under each plant. You'll use saucers to collect runoff water later. If you are using a camera, snap a "before" photo of each plant.

3 Pollute the water! Fill an empty 2-liter bottle with tap water. Pour it into the bucket. Add oil and Epsom salt. Mix with the stirrer until the salt dissolves. Add the soil-and-sand mixture, and stir.

Did you know...

Garbage dumped on beaches flutters into oceans. What happens when an endangered sea turtle spots a plastic bag bobbing in waves? The turtle mistakes the bag for a jellyfish, its favorite dinner, and gobbles it up. Sadly, the bag blocks the sea turtle's digestive tract and kills the turtle.

4 For seven days, water the plants. Each day, water Wetland 1 with the polluted mixture. On day one, water Wetland 2 with tap water.

5 Starting with day two, water Wetland 2 with runoff water from Wetland 1. Predict what will happen over the week. Make notes in your journal to describe outcomes. Where do oil and sediments collect? Which plant is affected first? Do your plants survive?

6 After seven days, assess your findings. How does polluted water impact wetland plant growth? If you took a "before" picture, snap an "after" one. Compare the images.

Supplies

- science journal and pencil
- 2 fern plants, approximately the same size
- permanent marker
- 2 stick-on labels
- 2 saucers
- ruler
- camera (optional)
- 2-liter bottle of tap water
- bucket
- ½ cup oil (118 milliliters)
- ¼ cup Epsom salt (60 grams)
- paint stirrer
- 1 cup of soil and sand mixed together (225 grams)

TEST BUTTERFLY FEEDERS

Climate change has impacted the number of butterflies in the wild. Build two feeders and see how many butterflies come to hang out. You'll probably see plenty of other insects come to your feeders, too. Look them up in a field guide to identify them.

I. JAR FEEDER

This is a simple butterfly feeder that you can make with a baby food jar and some sugar water.

Be Careful: Ask an adult for help with the hammer and nail.

1 Combine water and sugar (use tablespoons for a larger jar) in a saucepan. Boil until the sugar is dissolved. Let it cool.

2 Have an adult help you use the hammer and nail to make a small hole in the lid of the jar.

3 Cut a strip of the kitchen sponge and pull it through the hole in the lid, leaving about a half-inch sticking out from the top of the lid (1½ centimeters). The sponge must be a tight fit so the liquid doesn't drip. Put water in the jar to test it. If it leaks, try a bigger piece of sponge.

4 Make a hanger. Tie some string around the mouth of the jar. Cut two more lengths of string about 30 inches long (76 centimeters). Tie the end of one string around the string tied around the mouth of the jar. Attach the other end on the opposite side of the jar to make a loop. Tie the second length of string across from the first in the same way. Use one more piece of string to tie the tops of the loops together. Now turn the jar upside down and make sure it hangs steadily.

5 Decorate the jar with brightly colored construction paper (flower shapes are best) or artificial flowers. The "prettier" it is, the more it will attract butterflies!

Supplies

- 9 teaspoons water
- 1 teaspoon sugar
- small saucepan
- small jar with lid (like a baby food jar)
- hammer and nail
- kitchen sponge
- scissors
- ruler
- string
- construction paper or artificial flowers

6 Fill the jar with the cooled sugar water, screw the lid on tightly, and turn the jar upside down. Hang your feeder outside and wait for the butterflies to come!

Did you know...

A butterfly's tongue is specially adapted for a liquid diet. A proboscis is a built-in, tube-like tongue. It's like a straw! The butterfly uncoils the proboscis to suck up juicy nectar.

continues on next page . . .

II. SWEET BANANA FEEDER

Be Careful: Ask an adult to help you slice the banana and use the stove.

1 Peel and slice the banana. Place the slices into the bowl. Use the fork to mash them. Add sugar and water. Blend to create a paste.

2 Transfer the mixture to the saucepan. Simmer on the stovetop at low heat, stirring occasionally. Cook until the mixture is sticky. Remove from heat. Allow the mixture to cool completely.

3 Time for the serving tray! Use the paper punch to make three holes around the edges of the plate, forming a triangle. Cut string or yarn into three equal pieces. Thread each piece through a hole in the plate, and knot tightly.

4 Make sure the banana mixture is thoroughly cooled. Spread it on the plate for butterflies to feast on. Tie the feeder to a low-slung tree branch. Observe the kinds of butterflies that flit by for a sweet treat!

Supplies

- mushy banana
- knife
- mixing bowl
- fork
- 3 ounces unrefined sugar (100 grams)
- 8 ounces water (250 milliliters)
- saucepan
- stove
- wooden spoon
- paper punch
- paper plate
- scissors
- 3-4 feet string or yarn (about 1 meter)

Did you know...

Butterflies taste with their hind feet! Special taste receptors, or nerve endings, allow the insects to zone in on the perfect plant.

Glossary

acidic: bitter, tart, or sour.

adaptation: the changes a plant or animal has made to help it survive.

adapt: to change to survive in new or different conditions.

algae: plants that live mainly in water. They do not have leaves, roots, or stems.

amoeba: a bloblike single-celled organism. Plural is amoebae.

amphibian: a cold-blooded animal, such as a toad, frog or salamander, that needs sunlight to keep warm and shade to stay cool. Amphibians live on land and in the water.

anatomy: the internal structure of an organism.

anther: the flower part that produces and holds pollen.

antifreeze: a liquid that is added to a second liquid to lower the temperature at which the second liquid freezes.

aquatic: living or growing in water.

arthritis: a medical condition that causes swollen joints, stiffness, and pain.

asexual: reproduction without male and female cells joining.

atmosphere: the mixture of gases surrounding a planet.

atoms: tiny particles of matter that make up everything.

auxin: a chemical in a plant that causes leaves to bend and lengthen.

bacteria: single-celled organisms found in soil, water, plants, and animals. They help decay food and some bacteria are harmful. Singular is bacterium.

bioaccumulation: the buildup of harmful substances inside the tissues of living things.

biologist: a scientist who studies life.

biology: the study of life and of living organisms.

bioluminescence: a chemical reaction that allows fireflies to produce their own light.

biomagnification: the process through which harmful substances become more concentrated as they pass up a food chain.

biome: a natural area with a distinct climate, and with plants and animals adapted for life there. Deserts and rainforests are examples of biomes.

bog: a marshy wetland made of decomposing plants.

botanist: a scientist who studies plant life.

botany: the study of plants.

camouflage: the use of colors or patterns to blend in with a background.

cannibal: an animal that eats its own species.

carbohydrate: the sugar that is the source of food and energy in a plant.

carnivore: an animal that eats only other animals.

cell: the basic unit or part of a living thing. Cells are so small they can only be seen with a microscope.

cell wall: the part of a plant cell that gives shape to the cell.

chlorophyll: the chemical in a plant's cell that gives a plant its green color.

Glossary

chloroplasts: the parts of a plant cell in which sunlight is converted to energy.

chromosome: a rod-shaped structure in a cell nucleus that carries genes.

climate: average weather patterns in an area over many years.

colony: a group of plants or animals living cooperatively together.

congregation: a group of animals.

coniferous: describes cone-bearing shrubs and trees, often with needles for leaves. Coniferous trees do not lose their leaves each year.

conservationist: a person who works to preserve nature.

consumer: an organism that eats other organisms.

cotyledon: the first leaves produced by a seed.

cross-pollination: when pollen from one plant transfers to the stigma of another plant.

crude: very basic.

crustacean: an animal such as a crab or shrimp with a hard outer shell, jointed limbs, and two sets of antennae.

crystal: a solid with its **atoms** arranged in a geometric pattern.

cytoplasm: the gel-like inside of a cell.

debris: litter.

deciduous: describes plants and trees that shed their leaves each year.

decomposers: organisms such as ants, fungi, and worms that break down wastes, dead plants, and dead animals.

defense mechanism: a way to protect oneself.

dissect: to cut something apart to study what's inside.

diverse: lots of different kinds.

diversity: a range of different things.

dormant: not growing and developing.

dust mite: a microscopic insect that feeds on dead skin cells. Dust mites are a common cause of allergies.

ecosystem: a community of living and nonliving things and their **environments**.

electron: a particle in an atom with a negative charge.

embryo: a tiny plant inside a seed.

endangered: a plant or animal species with a dangerously low population.

endoplasmic reticulum: a network of membranes that makes changes and transports materials through the cell.`

environment: everything in nature, living and nonliving, including animals, plants, rocks, soil, and water.

evolve: to gradually develop over time and become more complex.

extinction: when a species dies out and there are no more left in the world.

fertile: describes soil that is good for growing crops.

fertilization: the joining of male sperm cells and female egg cells.

fertilize: to join female and male cells to produce seeds and offspring.

filament: the stalk that supports the anther.

fission: the splitting of a single-celled organism into two parts.

flammable: something that burns very easily.

food chain: a community of animals and plants where each is eaten by another higher up in the chain. Food chains combine into food webs.

fungi: molds, mushrooms, mildew, and rust. Singular is fungus.

genes: basic units in our cells that carry characteristics from one generation to the next.

geotropism: plant growth in response to the force of gravity, which makes the roots grow toward the earth.

germinate: to sprout and begin to grow.

gills: the part of a mushroom that contains spores.

glucose: the simple sugar that plants produce through photosynthesis.

Golgi bodies: sacs that receive proteins from the cell, put them together with other proteins, and send them around the cell.

gore: to pierce an animal's flesh.

gravity: a force that pulls all objects to the earth.

habitat: the natural area where a plant or animal lives.

herbivore: an animal that eats only plants.

hibernate: to sleep through the winter in a cave or underground.

hormone: a chemical in a plant that controls functions like plant growth and fruit ripening.

hypothesis: a prediction or unproven idea that tries to explain certain facts or observations.

ingest: to swallow.

instinct: an inborn behavior, need, or characteristic.

invasive species: a nonnative plant or animal that harms an ecosystem.

larva: the worm-like stage of an insect's life. Plural is larvae.

legume: a plant that has flowers and produces edible seeds, such as nuts, peas, soybeans, and lentils.

lichen: yellow, green, and gray plants that grow in patches on rocks. Lichen are made of algae and fungi.

life cycle: the growth and changes a living thing goes through, from birth to death.

lysosome: an organelle that aids in digestion.

malnutrition: poor nutrition caused by not eating the right foods.

mammal: a warm-blooded animal, such as a human, dog or cat, that can keep itself warm. Mammals feed milk to their young and usually have hair or fur covering most of their skin.

mate: to reproduce.

membrane: the outer layer of a cell that allows materials to pass in and out.

metamorphosis: an animal's complete change in physical form as it develops into an adult.

microbiology: the study of microorganisms.

microbiome: a tiny   .

microorganism: a tiny living thing, such as bacteria, that can only be seen with a microscope. Also called a microbe.

microscopic: something so small it can only be seen under a microscope.

migrate: to move from one environment to another when seasons change.

Glossary

mineral: a solid, nonliving substance found in the earth and in water.

mitochondria: the parts of the cell that change food into energy.

moss: a small seedless plant that grows in soft feathery patches in moist places, such as the ground of a thick forest.

multicelluar: made up of many cells.

naked eye: the human eye without help from a microscope.

natural selection: the process that allows organisms best adapted for an environment to reproduce.

nonnative: a plant or animal growing or living in an environment it didn't originally come from.

nucleus: the central part of a cell.

nutrient: a substance an organism needs to live and grow.

offspring: an animal's young.

omnivore: an animal that eats both plants and animals.

organ: a body part that has a certain function, such as the heart or kidneys.

organelle: a structure inside a cell that performs a special function or job.

organism: a living thing, such as a plant or animal.

ovary: the part of the pistil in a flower that bears ovules and ripens into a fruit.

overwinter: to survive the winter by remaining in an environment.

oviparous: an animal that lays eggs.

ovule: a small structure that develops into a seed after it joins with a grain of pollen.

oxygen: a gas you breathe to live.

parasite: a plant or animal that gets its nourishment from a host plant or animal, while also damaging the host.

peat: waterlogged, decomposed organic matter.

petals: the showy, brightly colored outer area of a flower.

photosynthesis: the process by which plants produce food, using light as energy.

phototropism: plant growth in response to light, which makes the leaves grow or bend toward a light source.

pigment: a substance that gives something its color.

pioneer: to be one of the first to discover something new.

pistil: the female, seed-producing reproductive part of a flower. It includes the ovary, style, and stigma.

pit: the hard seed of a fruit that has only one seed.

plaque: a sticky substance that forms on teeth and gums and causes decay.

plumule: the part of a plant embryo that forms a shoot.

pollen: a fine, yellow powder produced by flowering plants. Pollen fertilizes the seeds of other plants as it gets spread around by the wind, birds, and insects.

pollination: transferring male pollen to the female stigma.

pollinator: an insect or other animal that transfers pollen from the male part of a flower to the female part of a flower.

pore: a tiny opening through which substances pass.

116

predator: an animal that hunts another animal for food.

prey: an animal hunted and eaten by other animals.

producer: an organism that makes its own food.

projectile: to hurl, launch, or blast forward.

protoplasm: the colorless liquid that forms the living matter of a cell.

protozoa: one-celled microscopic organisms, such as an amoeba, that can divide only while living inside another organism. Singular is protozoon.

pseudopod: a foot-like bulge an amoeba uses to move.

rabies: a virus of the nervous system transmitted through the bite of an infected mammal.

radicle: the first part of a plant embryo that emerges and forms a root.

regurgitate: to throw up partially digested food to feed a baby.

remote: far-away and isolated.

reproduce: to make something new, just like itself. To have babies.

reptile: a cold-blooded animal, like a snake or lizard, that needs sunlight to keep warm and shade to stay cool. It crawls on its belly or on short legs.

revolutionize: to transform, or make a huge and complete change.

ribosomes: the protein builders of a cell.

root: the underground plant structure that anchors the plant and takes in water and minerals from soil.

scavenger: an animal, bird, or insect that eats rotting food or animals that are already dead.

sediment: loose rock particles such as sand or clay.

seed: the part of a plant that holds all the beginnings of a plant.

seed coat: the hard protective covering on a seed.

self-pollination: when a plant's pollen falls onto its own stigma.

sepals: the special leaves that enclose a flower.

sexual reproduction: reproduction that joins male and female cells.

species: a group of plants or animals that are closely related and look the same.

specimen: a sample of something.

sperm: the cell that comes from a male in the reproductive process.

spore: a structure produced by fungi that sprouts and grows into a new fungus.

stamen: the male, pollen-producing reproductive part of a flower. It includes the filament and anther.

Glossary

stem: the plant structure that supports leaves, flowers, and fruits.

stigma: the upper part of the pistil, which receives pollen.

stimulus: a change in an organism's environment that causes an action, activity, or response.

stockpile: to store large amounts of something for later use. Also called hoarding.

stomata: tiny pores on the outside of leaves that allow gases and water vapor to pass in and out.

stress: pressure or strain, often due to changes in conditions or environments.

style: the stalk-like tube that extends from the ovary to support the stigma.

symbiosis: the relationship between two different organisms, in which one or both benefit.

talon: a claw belonging to a bird of prey.

thigmotropism: the response of a plant to physical contact.

tissue: a large number of cells similar in form and function that are grouped together.

topsoil: the top layer of soil.

toxic: poisonous.

transpiration: the process by which plants give off water vapor and waste products.

tropism: a plant's involuntary response to a change in its environment.

unicellular: made of only one cell.

vacuole: a compartment in the cytoplasm of a plant cell that stores food and waste.

venomous: poisonous.

ventilate: to supply fresh air into a room or enclosed place.

viviparous: an animal that has live births.

warren: burrows where rabbits live.

water vapor: water as a gas, like steam, mist or fog.

wetland: an area where the land is soaked with water, such as a swamp.

zoology: the study of animals.

Resources

Books

- Bang, Molly and Penny Chisholm. *Living Sunlight: How Plants Bring the Earth to Life.* Nutmeg Media DVD, 2009.

- Bardhan-Quallan, Sudipta. *Nature Science Experiments: What's Hopping in a Dust Bunny?* Sterling, 2010.

- Cassie, Brian. *National Audubon Society First Field Guide to Trees* Scholastic, 1999.

- VanCleave, Janice. *A+ Projects in Biology: Winning Experiments for Science Fairs and Extra Credit.* John Wiley & Sons, 1993.

- VanCleave, Janice. *Biology for Every Kid: 101 Easy Experiments That Really Work.* John Wiley & Sons, 1990.

- *Eyewitness Plant.* DK Vision and BBC Worldwide Americas DVD, 1997.

- *Life Cycles (Bill Nye the Science Guy).* Disney Educational Productions DVD, 2004.

Web Sites

- **Backyard Nature** www.backyardnature.net/index.html

- **Cell Animations and Movies** publications.nigms.nih.gov/insidethecell/extras/index.html

- **For the Birds: U.S. Fish and Wildlife Service** publications.usa.gov/epublications/forbirds/forbird.htm

- **Life Cycle of the Red-eyed Tree Frog Video** video.nationalgeographic.com/video/animals/amphibians-animals/frogs-and-toads/frog_greentree_lifecycle/

- **Microbe Magic** microbemagic.ucc.ie/index.html

- **Microbe Zoo** commtechlab.msu.edu/sites/dlc-me/zoo/

- **Photosynthesis: Putting Together With Light** www.sites.ext.vt.edu/virtualforest/modules/photo.html

- **Science of Gardening** www.exploratorium.edu/gardening/feed/index.html

- **Humane Society of the United States** www.humanesociety.org/issues/exotic_pets/facts/

- **Smithsonian National Zoo: Just for Kids** nationalzoo.si.edu/audiences/kids/default.cfm?fonzref=kids.htm

- **Soil Science Education** soil.gsfc.nasa.gov/

Index

Index